Sales and Use Tax Answer Book
Second Edition

by Bruce M. Nelson, James T. Collins, John C. Healy, and Robert M. Kozub

Sales and Use Tax Answer Book provides detailed guidance on sales and use taxation. In the easy-to-use question and answer format, the authors identify and explain the critical issues, important compliance procedures, common problems and mistakes that arise when dealing with a sales and use tax problem. Providing expert practical advice, *Sales and Use Tax Answer Book* helps you obtain the most advantageous outcomes for your clients.

Highlights of the 2003 Supplement

The 2003 Supplement to *Sales and Use Tax Answer Book* brings you up to date on the latest developments in this complex and constantly changing area. Highlights include:

- New and expanded discussions of procedural due process issues;
- Updated charts and tables;
- Expanded discussion of the various tests for resale sales;
- Analysis of California's recent rulings against remote sellers Barnes & Noble.com and Borders Online; and

- A report on the ongoing progress of the Streamlined Sales Tax Project.

6/03

For questions concerning this shipment, billing, or other customer service matters, call our Customer Service Department at 1-800-234-1660.

For toll-free ordering, please call 1-800-638-8437.

A WoltersKluwer Company

Sales and Use Tax Answer Book

2003 Supplement

This supplement is to be used in conjunction with the Second Edition of *Sales and Use Tax Answer Book*

Sales and Use Tax Answer Book

2003 Supplement

Bruce M. Nelson, CPA
James T. Collins, JD
John C. Healy, MST, CPA
Robert M. Kozub, DBA, CPA

1185 Avenue of the Americas, New York, NY 10036
www.aspenpublishers.com

A Wolters Kluwer Company
www.aspenpublishers.com

Printed in the United States of America

ISBN 0-7355-3861-1

1 2 3 4 5 6 7 8 9 0

About Aspen Publishers

Aspen Publishers, headquartered in New York City, is a leading information provider for attorneys, business professionals, and law students. Written by preeminent authorities, our products consist of analytical and practical information covering both U.S. and international topics. We publish in the full range of formats, including updated manuals, books, periodicals, CDs, and online products.

Our proprietary content is complemented by 2,500 legal databases, containing over 11 million documents, available through our Loislaw division. Aspen Publishers also offers a wide range of topical legal and business databases linked to Loislaw's primary material. Our mission is to provide accurate, timely, and authoritative content in easily accessible formats, supported by unmatched customer care.

To order any Aspen Publishers title, go to *www.aspenpublishers.com* or call 1-800-638-8437.

To reinstate your manual update service, call 1-800-638-8437.

For more information on Loislaw products, go to *www.loislaw.com* or call 1-800-364-2512.

For Customer Care issues, e-mail *CustomerCare@aspenpublishers.com*; call 1-800-234-1660; or fax 1-800-901-9075.

Aspen Publishers
A Wolters Kluwer Company

SUBSCRIPTION NOTICE

This Aspen Publishers product is updated on a periodic basis with supplements to reflect important changes in the subject matter. If you purchased this product directly from Aspen Publishers, we have already recorded your subscription for the update service.

If, however, you purchased this product from a bookstore and wish to receive future updates and revised or related volumes billed separately with a 30-day examination review, please contact our Customer Service Department at 1-800-234-1660, or send your name, company name (if applicable), address, and the title of the product to:

Aspen Publishers
7201 McKinney Circle
Frederick, MD 21704

Preface

Forty-five states and the District of Columbia impose a sales tax on the retail sales of tangible personal property and selected services as well as a use tax on the storage, use, or consumption of tangible personal property and selected services. In addition to the states, some 7,500 cities, municipalities, towns, school districts, counties, and other special taxing districts levy sales and use taxes. The varying rates, the changing jurisdictional boundaries, the different tax bases, and the often inconsistent and contradictory interpretations of similarly worded statutes make sales and use tax compliance, let alone planning, staggeringly complex.

As this supplement goes to print, many states are facing their biggest fiscal crisis since the 1930s, ironically the decade in which state sales taxes first became a familiar and permanent part of the fiscal landscape. State reactions to the crisis include raising rates, reducing vendor fees, expanding the tax base, and aggressively pursuing out-of-state vendors that the states believe should be collecting and remitting sales and use tax. Nevertheless, the key questions continue to include:

- What types of sales are taxable?
- What items are exempt from tax?
- How are the rates applied?
- What kinds of deductions are allowed?
- How are specific businesses taxed?
- What costs are includible in the tax base?

This supplement addresses the above questions not only through updates to the book's many charts but also by incorporating recent court cases and expanding on perennially troublesome issues. For example, we have added new or expanded discussions of procedural due process, the various tests for resale sales, California's recent rulings against remote sellers Barnes & Noble.com and Borders Online, and the ongoing progress of the Streamlined Sales Tax Project. Our goal in the supplement, as with the book, remains the same—to provide the taxpayer, practitioner, or administrator a quick and authoritative guide to general sales and use tax principles, specific applications, and interpretations.

About the Authors

Bruce M. Nelson, MA, CPA, is a state and local tax consultant in Fort Collins, Colorado. Mr. Nelson earned a Bachelor of Arts degree from the University of Nebraska–Lincoln and a Master's degree from Colorado State University and is a certified public accountant in the state of Colorado. He is also on the adjunct faculty for Regis University where he teaches courses in individual, partnership, and corporate taxation. Mr. Nelson has worked in the state and local tax field for more than 20 years, first as a Senior Revenue Agent for the Colorado Department of Revenue and then as a Senior Tax Manager in Ernst & Young's Denver, Colorado, office. He is a frequent speaker and teaches continuing education classes in state and local tax for the University of Denver's Graduate Tax Program and the Colorado Society of CPAs. Mr. Nelson has published more than 30 tax articles in many publications, including *Journal of Accountancy, Tax Executive, Controller Magazine, Journal of Multistate Taxation, State Tax Notes,* and *Colorado Lawyer.* Mr. Nelson is a member of the American Institute of Certified Public Accountants and the Colorado Society of Certified Public Accountants, where he served on the State Tax Committee for four years.

James T. Collins, JD, is the executive director of the Deloitte and Touche Center for Multistate Taxation at the University of Wisconsin–Milwaukee. Mr. Collins earned a Bachelor of Science degree in political science and a Juris Doctor degree from the University of Georgia. In addition, Mr. Collins is an adjunct professor of taxation in the School of Business Administration at the Unviversity of Wisconsin–Milwaukee, where he has taught an interstate and local taxation course since 1980. He serves as the editor in chief and chairman of the editorial board of the *Journal of State Taxation* and as co-editor of the *Journal of Property Tax Management*. He was named the 1994 Corporate Wisconsin Tax Professional of the Year. Mr. Collins is the co-author of *State and Local Tax Answer Book*.

John C. Healy, MST, CPA, is the managing director of the Deloitte and Touche Center for Multistate Taxation and a lecturer in the Graduate Tax Program at the University of Wisconsin–Milwaukee and is co-editor of Aspen Publishers' *Multistate Corporate Tax Guide*. Mr. Healy has more than 20 years of state and local tax experience and has held SALT management positions at Miller Brewing Company and General Electric Medical Systems. He has a Bachelor of Science degree in accounting from Marquette University and a Master of Science degree in taxation from the University of Wisconsin—Milwaukee. He is also a certified public accountant. Mr. Healy has published numerous articles in professional tax journals and is a past recipient of IPT's Literary Award. He is also the author of *Surviving the Sales Tax Audit* in Commerce Clearing House's *Solutions for State and Local Taxation*. Mr. Healy has served as an instructor in a variety of continuing professional education and university tax courses. He is a member of the AICPA and WICPA and is past chair of the WICPA Wisconsin Taxation Committee.

Robert M. Kozub, DBA, CPA, is an Associate Professor of Taxation in the School of Business Administration at the University of Wisconsin–Milwaukee. Dr. Kozub is the Lawrence G. Regner Fellow in Accounting and Taxation and a faculty associate in the Deloitte and Touche Center for Multistate Taxation at the University of Wisconsin–Milwaukee. He earned his Doctor of Business Administration degree from the University of Kentucky. Professor Kozub is a certified public accountant in the state of Wisconsin. Dr. Kozub is a member of the Editorial Advisory Board of the *Journal of State Taxation* and the *Journal of Property Tax Management*. He has published more than 125 articles in scholarly and professional accounting, business, and taxation journals, such as the *Journal of the American Taxation Association*, the *Journal of Taxation*, the *Journal of State Taxation*, the *Journal of Property Tax Management*, and *Corporate Taxation*. In addition, Professor Kozub has contributed to a number of books, including *Multistate Corporate Tax Almanac*, *Multistate Tax Guide to Flow-Through Entities*, and *State and Local Tax Answer Book*.

Acknowledgments

While reading a book is a particularly solitary and individual experience, producing one is not. Aside from the authors, there are proofreaders, copy editors, graphic designers, printers, bookbinders and a host of others in publishing, marketing, and distributing a book. Obviously, we cannot thank everyone individually, but we would like to say a special thank you to Carol Kizer, Susan Chazin, Sue Frayman, Rosemary DeStefano, and Lina Carmona for their work and assistance on this book. Jim wishes to thank his wife, Elizabeth, and his children, James, Lachlan, Ivy, and Wylly, for their support, since 1965, of his multistate tax practice, teaching, and writing. John wishes to thank his wife, Jackie, and their children, Jessica and James, for their patience, support, and understanding during the production of this book and throughout his career. Bruce would also like to thank Ted Middle and Mark Kozik of Ernst & Young LLP for all they have taught him over the years and his wife, Kathy, and daughter, Laura, for pretending to be interested.

How to Use This Supplement

The *Sales and Use Tax Answer Book, 2003 Supplement,* updates questions contained in the Second Edition. The supplement includes new or expanded discussions of procedural due process, the various tests for resale sales, and California's recent rulings against remote sellers Barnes & Noble.com and Borders Online, as well as the ongoing progress of the Streamlined Sales Tax Project.

Organizationally, this book parallels the structure of the Second Edition, providing supplemental material where change has occurred. The following overview explains how this easy-to-use volume provides information on sales and use taxation.

List of Questions. A detailed list of questions follows the table of contents in the front of the book in order to help the reader locate areas of immediate interest. This list provides both the question number and the page number on which the question appears. A series of subheadings helps to group and organize the question by topic within each chapter.

Question Numbers. To make the *Supplement* easy to use in conjunction with the main volume, whenever a question from the main volume is updated, it is repeated in its entirety in the *Supplement.* The *Supplement* also uses a point system to number new questions, permitting new material to be immediately identified with related material from the main volume, so that the overall organization of the main volume is preserved.

Index. This index references only the supplement.

Contents

CHAPTER **21**

List of Questions

Chapter 2 Constitutional Rights

Chapter 3 Taxable Persons

Chapter 4 Taxable Transactions

Chapter 5 Interstate and Extraterritorial Transactions

Taxing Local Activity

Taxability of Property Purchased or Leased in One State and Used in Another

Interstate Sales Taxation of Telecommunications Services

Mailing Lists

Internet or Electronic Commerce

Chapter 6 Subjects of Sales and Use Taxes

Tangible Personal Property

Self-Constructed Assets

Computer Software

Containers and Packing Materials

Leased Property

Machinery and Equipment

Mergers, Consolidations, Acquisitions, Liquidations, or Incorporations

Drop Shipments

Pollution Control Equipment

Construction Contractors

Clothing

Chapter 9 Rates of Tax

Chapter 10 Returns or Reports

Chapter 11 Payment

Chapter 17 Collection of Tax by Seller

Passing On or Absorbing the Tax

Collection by Out-of-State Sellers

Chapter 19 Penalties

Penalties

Interest

Chapter 21 Sales Tax Reform and the Streamlined Sales Tax Project

The Streamlined Sales Tax Project

Chapter 2

Constitutional Rights

The U.S. Constitution and all state constitutions contain restrictions on the nature and scope of state and local taxation. This chapter discusses those restrictions. Currently, the two most important U.S. constitutional restrictions on state and local tax are the Due Process and Commerce Clauses. Other U.S. constitutional issues affecting state and local taxation include the Equal Protection, Privileges and Immunities, and Supremacy Clauses. Most state constitutions contain similar provisions, often adding others such as uniformity and equality standards. The Due Process Clause, whose roots can be traced back to the Magna Carta (1215), concerns itself with questions of fundamental fairness between a government and those over whom the government seeks jurisdiction. The Commerce Clause imposes restrictions on states with regard to interstate commerce. The Equal Protection Clause of the Fourteenth Amendment prohibits states from arbitrary or capricious discrimination. The Privileges and Immunities Clause, found in both the Fourth and Fourteenth Amendments, prohibits states from discriminating against citizens of other states. Because corporations are not citizens, the Privileges and Immunities Clauses have had limited application in the sales and use tax area. The Supremacy Clause places restrictions upon the states' power to tax either the federal government or its agents. State uniformity and equality clauses define acceptable distinctions among classes of taxpayers, property, or methodologies of assessment. In addition to general constitutional guidelines and prohibitions, this chapter also covers specific applications of constitutional issues with respect to government contractors, bankruptcies, national banks, taxation of Native Americans, the First Amendment issue, and statutory construction.

Due Process Clause

Q 2:1 What is the Due Process Clause?

The Fourteenth Amendment to the U.S. Constitution states:

> [Nor] shall any State deprive any person of life, liberty, or property, without due process of law . . . . [U.S. Const. amend. XIV, §1]

Due process is concerned with fundamental questions of fairness between a state and its citizens. Due process can be procedural, which is concerned with administrative fairness, or it can be substantive, which concerns itself with inalienable individual liberties. Put another way, procedural due process is concerned with how government acts, substantive due process with whether or not it has the right to act. For example, reading a suspect his or her rights when arrested is an example of procedural due process. Whether or not there exists under constitutional law a right to privacy is an example of substantive due process.

One of the key procedural state and local tax due process issues is "pay-to-play." States such as California, Illinois, New Mexico, North Carolina, and Pennsylvania require that a taxpayer pay an assessment before appealing it. For example, the California Court of Appeals recently ruled that it lacked jurisdiction to hear a taxpayer's challenge to a sales and use tax assessment because the taxpayer had failed to pay the tax owed. The taxpayer argued that to pay the assessment, which exceeded $1 million, would drive it into bankruptcy. Thus, the state was denying the company "its due process right to an administrative or judicial hearing by conditioning its right to a hearing on its payment of the full amount of the tax assessment." [J&D Auto Sales Inc. v. Klehs, No. B158932 (Court of Appeal, 2nd App. Dist., Mar. 14, 2003)] (Substantive due process is discussed in Q 2:2.)

Commerce Clause

Q 2:6 What is nexus?

Nexus is a term of art used in state and local taxation, referring to the links, connections, or contacts (both quantitative and qualitative) between a political jurisdiction and a taxpayer. If a taxpayer has sufficient nexus with a state, it will usually be deemed to be "doing business" in that state and be liable for that state's taxes. In short, nexus determines whether or not a company has to register and begin complying with a state's tax laws.

Nexus varies by type of tax. For sales tax nexus, generally all that is needed is more than a minimal physical presence in the state. The physical presence can be created by employees, independent contractors, or the ownership or leasing of property in the state. The physical presence of employees alone will not necessarily create nexus for income tax. Under federal legislation Public Law (P.L.) 86-272, nexus will not be created for income tax purposes by an employee or independent contractor if the person is doing no more than solicitation of sales of tangible personal property and the sales orders are being accepted and fulfilled from outside the state. (See Question 2:8.)

On October 17, 2002, the Multistate Tax Commission (MTC) approved a proposal that urges the states to adopt a new uniform nexus standard applicable to both sales and income taxes. Under the new proposal, "business activity" tax nexus would be created if, during the tax year, a company (1) owns in the state more than $50,000 in property; (2) incurs more than $50,000 in payroll; (3) generates more than $500,000 in sales; or (4) exceeds 25 percent of total property, total payroll, or total sales in the state.

Adoption of the new standard will require Congress to repeal P.L. 86-272 and address the constitutional restrictions enunciated by the U.S. Supreme Court in *Quill* and *National Bellas Hess*. In addition, the Streamlined Sales Tax Project (SSTP) may alter what constitutes nexus for sales and use tax purposes as states seek to simplify the tax collection process. (See Chapter 21 for a more thorough discussion of the SSTP.)

Planning Point 2-2. Because of the differing nexus standards for sales and use and income tax, it is feasible for a taxpayer to have sales tax nexus (employees in the state soliciting sales provides physical presence) but not have income tax nexus (solicitation of sales of tangible personal property where the shipment comes from stock located outside the state as a protected activity under P. L. 86-272 [15 U.S.C. §§ 381–384]). However, taxpayers with income tax nexus would be expected to have sales tax nexus, because the threshold test for sales tax nexus is lower (mere physical presence) than for income tax nexus. Taxpayers engaged in multistate activities should monitor their operations and activities constantly to avoid inadvertently triggering nexus. With the downturn of the economy and resulting downsizing that has occurred in recent years, taxpayers also may want to evaluate whether activities in a state are still sufficient to constitute nexus. For example, if an office or division has been closed, the taxpayer may no longer have sufficient nexus for the state to require collection of the sales tax.

Q 2:7 What constitutes nexus for sales and use tax purposes?

The U.S. Supreme Court held in *Quill* that physical presence was to be the bright-line test for sales and use tax nexus. If a seller has no physical presence in the state, it cannot be required to collect tax on its sales into the state. The debate since *Quill* has revolved around the following two questions:

1. How much physical presence is sufficient to create nexus?
2. Can nexus be attributed to the seller through the physical presence of the seller's agent or affiliate?

Physical presence. The U.S. Supreme Court has stated that physical presence must be more than the "slightest presence" to rise to a "standard of constitutional nexus." [National Geographic Soc'y v. California Bd. of Equalization, 430 U.S. 551, 556 (1977)] For example, in *Quill* the Court held that *Quill's* ownership of some floppy disks in North Dakota did not create sales and use tax nexus in the state. The disks, while owned by Quill, were software used by its customers to place orders and check current inventories and prices.

It is difficult to say with certainty how much physical presence will create the necessary "substantial nexus" to satisfy the Commerce Clause. Prior to *Quill,* in *Miller Bros. Co. v. Maryland* [347 U.S. 340 (1954)], the U.S. Supreme Court ruled that occasional deliveries, in its own trucks by a Delaware retailer into Maryland, did not create nexus for sales and use tax. After *Quill,* the Court had an opportunity to revisit the delivery issue in *Brown's Furniture, Inc. v. Wagner* [171 Ill. 2d 410, *cert. denied,* 519 U.S. 866 (1996)] but declined. The Illinois Supreme Court held that Brown's Furniture had nexus in Illinois by virtue of its advertising in the state coupled with 942 deliveries in its own trucks over a 10-month period. Such activity created nexus, the court said, because it was more than incidental, occasional, or sporadic, but instead "regular and frequent." More recently, the Illinois Appellate Court ruled that 30 furniture deliveries over a 26-month period was enough physical presence to be "substantial nexus" for sales and use tax. [Town Crier, Inc. v. Illinois, 315 Ill. App. 3d 286, 733 N.E.2d 780 (2000)]

State courts also have differed on whether occasional or sporadic visits by employees are sufficient physical presence to constitute "substantial nexus." New York has held that visits by an out-of-state retailer's employees can be more than the "slightest presence" required, creating nexus. In one case, the visits were to 19 wholesalers, four times a year, and in another, there were 41 visits over a three-year period. According to the New York court, an out-of-state company's presence "need not be substantial"; it need only be more than the "slightest presence." [Orvis Co. v. Tax Appeals Tribunal, 86 N.Y.2d 165, 654 N.E.2d 954, *cert. denied,* and Vermont Info. Processing, Inc. v. Tax Appeals Tribunal, 86 N.Y.2d 165, 654 N.E.2d 954, *cert. denied,* 516 U.S. 989 (1995)] In a holding to the contrary, the Kansas Supreme Court ruled that 11 visits by an out-of-state seller to install card readers did not create nexus, because the visits were isolated and sporadic. [*In re* Appeal of Intercard, Inc., 270 Kan. 346, 14 P.3d 1111 (2000)]

The physical presence need not be that of an employee or independent contractor. North Carolina is attempting to hold a company responsible for sales tax and corporate income and franchise taxes, whose only connection with the state is the selling and renting of VHS videotapes through the mail. Educational Resources, Inc. (ERI), a South Carolina company, sells and rents videotapes about workplace safety. Between 1990 and 1995 it made 219 sales and 906 rentals into North Carolina totaling $201,304 and $99,521 respectively. ERI did not have any employees in North Carolina or any other contacts with the state except for the tapes that it sold and rented to North Carolina customers through the mail. The tapes rented for $150 to $200. Customers would keep rented tapes between five and thirty days before mailing them back to ERI.

The North Carolina Department of Revenue audited ERI and assessed them for sales, income, and franchise taxes. North Carolina argued that the presence of the rented tapes, which were ERI's property, created nexus with the state. The Superior Court ruled in favor of ERI stating that "the Court finds and concludes that, under the Commerce Clause of the United States Constitution as interpreted in *Quill* . . . , and other cases, there is not a 'substantial nexus' justifying the state's attempts to collect the use tax, corporate income tax, and franchise tax in these cases." [Educational Resources, Inc. v. Tolson, Nos. 00CVS14723 and 14724, Wake County, (North Carolina Superior Court, Feb. 20, 2003)] As the reader may recall, the U.S. Supreme Court ruled in *Quill* that the licensing of its software in the state along with the presence of a few floppy disks did not constitute "substantial nexus." North Carolina has indicated that it will appeal the decision.

Attendance at trade shows and seminars also raises questions about the quantity and quality of physical presence as the test for substantial nexus. Some states are beginning to create safe-harbor exemptions from sales and use tax for limited participation in conventions and trade shows. For example, California regulations provide that out-of-state retailers may receive up to $10,000 in sales at up to 15 days of trade shows, seminars, or conventions without incurring any sales or use tax collection responsibilities. [Cal. Code Regs. tit. 18, § 1684] Minnesota also provides a similar, but more restrictive safe harbor of three days over 12 months. The Florida Supreme Court in *Florida v. Share International, Inc.* [676 So. 2d 1362 (Fla. 1996)] held that an annual three-day seminar was insufficient physical presence to create "substantial nexus." The court believed a more permanent presence was needed and that "without a continuing physical presence, the assessment of a tax against the mail order activities is unjustified and violated the Commerce Clause." Most states, however, do not provide such exemptions or safe harbors and aggressively pursue taxpayers with any physical presence in the state. Arguments continue between tax practitioners, revenue officials, and other commentators over whether or not the "substantial nexus" test for purposes of the Commerce Clause means substantial *physical* presence.

Affiliation, attribution, and agency. In addition to the continuing debate over physical presence, there is question as to whether or not the physical presence of a third party will create substantial nexus for an out-of-state taxpayer. The fact that the third party is an independent contractor may be irrelevant. What is at issue is the nature of the contractor's activities. As long ago as 1960, the U.S. Supreme Court held that independent contractors could create nexus for an out-of-state retailer. "The test," according to the Supreme Court, "is simply the nature and extent of the activities" in the state. Where there is "continuous local solicitation" with the independent contractors performing the same role and functions as sales employees, the out-of-state seller has nexus with the state. [Scripto v. Carson, 362 U.S. 207, 208 (1960)]

More recently, the Kansas Supreme Court found that independent sales representatives (ISRs) triggered nexus for the state's compensating use tax. The Court held that there was no constitutionally significant difference between the independent contractors assigned territories in *Scripto* and the undefined territories of the taxpayer's ISRs. [In the Matter of the Appeal of Family of Eagles, Ltd., No. 88118 (Kan. Sup. Ct., Apr. 18, 2003)]

If a third party acts as an agent for an out-of-state seller, that agency relationship may create nexus for the seller. A series of cases involving high school book club sales is illustrative: *Scholastic Book Clubs v. State Board of Equalization* [207 Cal. App. 2d 734 (1st Dist. 1989) (out-of-state book club is deemed to have nexus because teachers collected money from the schoolchildren)]; *Pledger v. Troll*

Book Clubs Inc. [871 S.W.2d 389 (Ark. 1994) (teachers are not agents for the out-of-state book seller)]; *Scholastic Book Clubs v. Michigan Department of Treasury* [567 N.W.2d 692 (Mich. Ct. App. 1997) (taxpayer does not have nexus, because teachers, lacking the authority to bind Scholastic, are not agents of Scholastic)]; and *In re Scholastic Book Clubs, Inc.* [920 P.2d 947 (Kan. 1996) (Kansas Supreme Court holds that Scholastic has nexus, because an agency relationship exists with the schoolteachers)]. Although the differing conclusions of these cases indicate the importance of a state's specific interpretation of its laws on agency, the cases remain troubling because substantial nexus can be created by a third party in absence of a formal contract or compensation.

A secondary issue related to the use of independent contractors and the law of agency is whether activities unrelated to sales or solicitation will also constitute substantial nexus. For example, will the performance of post-sale services by independent contractors create nexus for an out-of-state seller? The Multistate Tax Commission's Nexus Program Bulletin 95-1 generated considerable discussion when it was issued, because it asserted that warranty repair services provided by third-party independent contractors created nexus for an out-of-state seller. More than 20 states have adopted the Bulletin. New York has held that an independent third party engaged by an out-of-state seller to diagnose and repair computers sold in-state by the seller created nexus for the seller. [TSB-A-00 (42) S (N.Y. Dep't of Taxation Fin. Oct. 13, 2000)]

Connecticut recently used the Multistate Tax Commission's Bulletin 95-1 in its unsuccessful attempt to assert that Dell Catalog Sales had nexus with the state. Dell sold computer service contracts that were to be fulfilled by an independent third party, BancTec, with whom Dell had an exclusive contract. Although the court found that BancTec was an independent contractor operating on Dell's behalf, it held that the "missing ingredient" in determining whether Dell had nexus was the "frequency, if any, of the number of on-site service calls." In other words, Connecticut failed to show that BancTec, Dell's independent third-party contractor, "had sufficient substantive physical presence in the state" to create nexus. "Isolated and sporadic physical contacts are insufficient to establish a substantial nexus [with] Connecticut." [Dell Catalog Sales v. Comm'r of Rev. (Conn. Super. Ct., Judicial Dist. of New Britain, July 10, 2003)]

With the growth in e-commerce, states have taken opposing positions on whether locating a server in the state creates more than the "slightest presence" needed to create nexus. States are still sorting out the nexus issues surrounding the presence of servers in managed hosting and co-location service providers.

States have been routinely unsuccessful in arguing that the physical presence of an out-of-state seller's affiliate creates nexus for the out-of-state taxpayer. Generally, the states have tried to argue that the affiliate had an agency relationship with the out-of-state vendor, because the two shared the same business names, trademarks, and logos, engaged in cross advertising, or were in similar lines of business. For example, Bloomingdale's had different affiliated corporate entities conducting sales in Pennsylvania, one through in-state retail stores, the other through mail-order catalog. Pennsylvania argued that the mail-order company had nexus because its corporate affiliate's in-state stores sold many of the same goods, shared advertising campaigns, and on two occasions accepted merchandise returns of items purchased by catalog. The Pennsylvania Commonwealth Court found for the taxpayer, rejecting the state's argument that nexus existed because of an agency relationship between the affiliated corporations. [Bloomingdale's By Mail, Ltd. v. Department of Rev., 567 A.2d 773 (Pa. Commw. Ct. 1989), *aff'd without opinion*, 591 A.2d 1047 (Pa. 1991)] The courts came to similar conclusions in two cases with Saks Fifth Avenue. [SFA Folio Collections Inc. v. Bannon, 217 Conn. 220 (1990), 585 A.2d 666 (Conn. 1991); SFA Folio Collections Inc. v. Tracy, 652 N.E.2d 693 (Ohio 1995)] The Ohio case is of particular interest because the state attempted to use the income tax "unitary" doctrine to assert substantial nexus for sales tax. *See* the section on "Unitary Theory" in James T. Collins & Robert M. Kozub, State and Local Taxation Answer Book, ch. 10 (Aspen Publishers 2000).

California continues to be one of the state leaders in asserting nexus through agency and affiliation. The California State Board of Equalization (SBE) recently ruled in two separate hearings that an online bookseller with no physical presence in the state must collect the state's use tax.

Borders Online, Inc., operates a web site through which it sells primarily books, CDs, and DVDs. It is a separate corporate entity affiliated with the traditional "bricks and mortar" Borders, Inc. bookstores. Borders, Inc., bookstores routinely accepted returns from its patrons regardless of whether the item was purchased at Borders, Inc., Borders Online, Inc., or one of Borders' competitors. If the item was purchased from a competitor, Borders, Inc., would give the purchaser store credit. If the item was purchased from Borders Online, the store would provide a cash refund.

The SBE determined that the refunding of cash for returned goods made Borders, Inc., the "authorized representative" of Borders Online. In addition, the SBE held that the refunding of cash for returns was a key element of the selling process and, in and of itself, constituted "selling" in California under California Revenue & Taxation Code (CRTC) § 6203. [Borders Online, Inc., SC OHA 97-638364 56270, (Cal. State Bd. of Equal., Sept. 26, 2001)]

The decision has been roundly criticized by the tax community who have argued that Borders' return policy was nothing more than good customer service rather than an action taken as a representative on behalf of Borders Online. Furthermore critics say, the SBE decision did not adequately address the principle articulated in *Scripto* and *Tyler Pipe* that an in-state representative creates nexus only through actions that purposefully establish and maintain a market in the state for the remote seller. [Scripto Inc. v. Carson, 362 U.S. 207 (1960) and Tyler Pipe Industries Inc. v. Washington, 483 U.S. 232 (1987)]

One year after its ruling in Borders Online, the SBE held that the online subsidiary of Barnes & Noble Booksellers, Inc. (B&N) had nexus in California because B&N distributed discount coupons that could be redeemed with its online affiliate Barnes & Noble.com (B&N.C). As in the Borders decision, the SBE determined that B&N acted as B&N.C's representative through their joint marketing effort whereby B&N.C paid to have printed coupons inserted into the shopping bags of B&N customers. The SBE rejected the taxpayer's argument that the discount coupons inserted into shoppers' bags were simply advertising akin to coupon inserts in magazines and newspapers. [Barnes & Noble.com, No. 89872 (Cal. State Bd. Equal., Sept. 12, 2002)]

New York recently issued an Advisory Opinion detailing that the operations of an instate retailer will not necessarily create nexus for an affiliated mail order company. The key to successfully preventing the presence of the instate retailer triggering nexus for the mail order company is to make certain that the retailer perform no services for the related mail order company. Actions that would trigger nexus attribution included customer referrals, accepting merchandise returns, accepting or fulfilling sales ordered from the catalog company, and distributing catalogs or catalog discount coupons on behalf of the mail order company. In addition, the Opinion went on to say that sharing a common inventory, common accounting and legal staff, or commingling advertising or solicitation activities would constitute evidence that the companies are "alter egos of each other" and thus each have nexus in New York. [Bass Pro Outdoor World, LLC (Adv. Op.) N.Y. Comm'r Tax'n and Fin., TSB-A-03(25)S (June 11, 2003)]

Tennessee's recent attempt to tax the activities of America Online has been stalled by the state's court of appeals who, pointing out that physical presence for nexus is fact-specific, has remanded the decision for further discovery. [America Online Inc. v. Johnson, No. 97-3786-III (Tenn. Chancery Ct., March 13, 2001), *rev'd and remanded,* America Online Inc. v. Johnson, M2001-00927-COA-R#-CV (Tenn. Ct. App. July 30, 2002)]

Instead of litigation, other states have simply passed legislation providing that companies are taxable in the state through affiliation. Effective January 1, 2002 a remote seller affiliated with an Arkansas retailer will have nexus with the state for the purposes of sales and use tax. The out-of-state or remote seller will have to collect and remit Arkansas use tax on sales into the state, if the seller is affiliated with an Arkansas retailer and "the vendor sells the same or substantially similar line of products . . . under the same or substantially similar business name, or the facilities or employees of the Arkansas retailer are used to advertise or promote sales by the vendor to Arkansas purchasers." [Ark. Code Ann. § 26-53-124(a)(3)(B)]

Like Arkansas, Minnesota has amended its statutes to require that an affiliated remote seller of an in-state retailer must collect the state's use tax. An out-of-state retailer or remote seller is an affiliate of an in-state entity if "the entity uses its facilities or employees in this state to advertise, promote, or facilitate the establishment or maintenance of a market for sales of items by the retailer to purchasers in this state or for the provision of services to the retailer's purchasers in this state, such as accepting returns of purchases for the retailer, providing assistance in resolving customer complaints of the retailer, or providing other services." [Minn. Stat. § 297A.66(4)]

Effective August 1, 2003, new legislation in Alabama provides that a remote seller has substantial nexus if (1) the instate and out-of-state vendors are related entities, and (2) the vendors use identical or substantially similar names and trade names, or share a contingent fee arrangement based on sales volume, or share a common business plan. [H650 (Act 390)]

Whether Arkansas', Minnesota's, or Alabama's new statutes will stand constitutional scrutiny remains to be seen.

Planning Point 2-2.1. As the previous discussion highlights, taxpayers with related parties engaging in substantially similar lines of business need to carefully evaluate what activities create nexus in each state in which they are doing business along with the relevant statutes and court cases in that state. Until further clarification comes in the form of a U.S. Supreme Court decision or federal legislation in this area, states will continue to enforce conflicting and, at times, contradictory provisions.

Planning Point 2-3. State sales tax statutes of limitations do not begin to toll until a return is filed. Consequently, unregistered taxpayers with nexus in a state are open to assessment for as many years as the state can establish a connection. This could be for a substantially longer period of time than the typical statute of limitations (three or four years in most states). In addition to the tax due, taxpayers also would owe penalties and interest on the delinquent amounts. The problem can be further exacerbated by the taxpayer's inability to enforce claims on former customers. Therefore, the seller may be forced to pay tax that could have been passed along to customers, resulting in unnecessary additional expense for the seller.

Equal Protection Clause

Q 2:12 Has the Equal Protection Clause been used frequently to overturn state tax laws?

No. Generally, the Supreme Court has prohibited only discrimination between subjects or taxpayers in the same class. As long as the distinctions drawn between subjects or classes are rationally related to a legitimate state purpose and not arbitrary, they would be upheld. If the "classification is neither capricious nor arbitrary, and rests upon some reasonable consideration of difference or policy, there is no denial of the equal protection of the law." [Brown-Forman Co. v. Collector of Revenue, 101 So. 2d 70 (La. 1958), *appeal dismissed,* 359 U.S. 28 (1959)] Thus, distinguishing between nonresidents and residents with respect to a state's sales and use tax is unconstitutional [Williams v. Vermont, 472 U.S. 14 (1985)], but taxing real property differently from tangible personal property is not. [Ohio Oil Co. v. Conway, 281 U.S. 146 (1930)]

The state of Vermont recently denied a claim that a real estate guide qualified for the state's use tax exemption for newspapers. Picket Fence Preview is a for-sale-by-owner publication listing real estate for sale. In addition, the guide also printed feature articles and community notices of interest to those buying and selling real estate. Picket Fence claimed that it met Vermont's definition of a newspaper. Thus, according to Picket Fence, to deny its claim to the use tax exemption while allowing it to publish newspapers violated its rights both under the Equal Protection Clause and the First Amendment.

The Vermont Supreme Court held that the publication did not meet the definition of a newspaper. Furthermore, there was no Equal Protection violation because the state's distinction between newspapers and other publications rested upon a legitimate interest in encouraging widespread, inexpensive distribution of the news. Finally, the Court held that since the determination of what constituted a newspaper in Vermont was not content-based, there was no First Amendment free speech violation. [*In re* Picket Fence Preview, 795 A.2d 1242 (Vermont, Mar. 22, 2002)]

"Suspect classifications" such as race, religion, gender, or political and civil rights such as the right to vote, receive stricter scrutiny than do tax classifications in recognition that the latter are necessary for the existence of the state. Taxes tied to "suspect classifications," however, will also face increased scrutiny. See, for example, the declaration that the payment of poll taxes as a condition of voting is unconstitutional. [Harper v. Virginia Bd. of Elections, 383 U.S. 663 (1966)]

Liquidation Sales in Bankruptcy

Q 2:24 Can states levy sales and use taxes on bankruptcy liquidation sales?

Yes. Although the authority to establish uniform bankruptcy laws rests with the U.S. Congress [U.S. Const. art. 1, § 8, cl. 4], the U.S. Supreme Court has ruled that the assessment of sales and use tax on bankruptcy sales is constitutional. [California State Bd. of Equalization v. Sierra Summit, Inc., 488 U.S. 992 (1989)] Because the purchaser pays the sales tax, the tax neither discriminates nor imposes an unconstitutional burden upon the federal bankruptcy courts or trustees. The trustee is not an agent for nor does it represent the federal government. Instead, the trustee represents the debtor.

Debtors in Washington must pay that state's use tax on the sale of assets made in anticipation or contemplation of bankruptcy. Although the federal bankruptcy code exempts such transfers from "stamp or similar tax," Washington's use tax did not qualify as a "similar tax." [*In re* GST Telecom, Inc., No. 00-1982 GMS (Bankr. Del. March 20, 2002)]

Taxation of Indians or Native Americans

Q 2:28 May a state impose its sales and use taxes on Native American reservations?

Maybe. Neither the basis nor the scope of Native Americans' tax immunity is clear. Tax immunity has been claimed based upon the Commerce Clause, tribal sovereignty, past treaties, and the unique historical relationship of the Native Americans and the creation of their reservations. Generally, if the legal incidence of the sales tax falls on the tribe or its members within the reservation, it is disallowed. In sum, on reservations, states may tax sales between non–Native Americans and sales by Native Americans to non–Native Americans, but not sales between Native Americans. Outside the reservations, individual tribal members generally must pay sales tax upon their purchases. According to the U.S. Supreme Court, "[A]bsent cession of jurisdiction or other federal statutes permitting it . . . a state is without power to tax reservation lands and reservation

Indians." [Oklahoma Tax Comm'n v. Chickasaw Nation, 515 U.S. 450, 458 (1995) (quoting County of Yakima v. Confederated Tribes and Bands of Yakima Nation, 502 U.S. 251, 258 (1992) (citation omitted)). *See also* Yavapai-Prescott Indian Tribe v. Scott, No. 96-16416 (9th Cir. June 30, 1997).] "In the special area of state taxation of Indian tribes . . . the [Court] has adopted a per se rule" prohibiting state jurisdiction. [California v. Cabazon Band of Mission Indians, 480 U.S. 202, 215 n. 17 (1987)] But as mentioned above, application of the per se rule depends on the tax's legal incidence. Therefore, taxes may not be generally imposed directly upon a tribe itself, but rather upon its non–Native American customers.

Several states have issued specific rulings detailing different kinds of transactions and the circumstances under which those transactions are taxable or exempt. (For some helpful examples, see the recent rulings in Connecticut and Kansas.) [Conn. Ruling No. 2002-3 (April 15, 2002) and Kan. Ruling 19-2002-1 (August 5, 2002)]

First Amendment Issues

Q 2:29 How does the First Amendment protection of free speech affect sales and use taxation?

The First Amendment to the U.S. Constitution provides that "Congress shall make no law . . . abridging the freedom of speech, or of the press . . . "[U.S. Const. amend. I]. Challenges to sales and use tax under the First Amendment generally arise from the belief that the tax in some way impedes free speech or favors one form of communication over another. The U.S. Supreme Court ruled that a Minnesota use tax imposed on newspaper purchases of ink and paper in excess of $100,000 annually violated the right to free speech by singling out newspapers for special treatment. The Supreme Court said, "Minnesota's ink and paper tax violated the First Amendment not only because it singles out the press, but also because it targets a small group of newspapers." [Minneapolis Star & Tribune Co. v. Commissioner of Revenue, 460 U.S. 575 (1983)]

The Supreme Court also overturned an Arkansas sales tax that taxed general-interest magazines while exempting professional, trade, religious, and sports publications. The Arkansas sales tax imposed on subscriptions to general magazines but not on subscriptions to newspapers or religious, professional, trade, and sport journals, violated the First Amendment right to free speech. The Arkansas tax discriminated against a "small group of magazines," and what was most disturbing was that "the Arkansas statute requires official scrutiny of [the] publication's content as the basis for imposing a tax." [Arkansas Writers' Project, Inc. v. Rugland, 481 U.S. 221 (1987)] The Court went on to say that there is no First Amendment prohibition against broad-based nondiscriminatory taxes—for example, if newspapers or magazines were to be taxed under a sales tax applicable to all retail sales of tangible personal property. In fact, in a later case, the U.S. Supreme Court ruled that disparate taxation of media such as cable, satellites, and newspapers was permissible, because the tax was of general application and did not distinguish itself based on content. The First Amendment does not prohibit discrimination in taxation "unless the tax is directed at, or presents the danger of suppressing, particular ideas." [Leathers v. Medlock, 499 U.S. 439 (1991)]

State supreme courts have followed the U.S. Supreme Court's lead in looking to discrimination in content for free speech violations. The state of Vermont recently denied a claim that a real estate guide qualified for the state's use tax exemption for newspapers. Picket Fence Preview is a for-sale-by-owner publication listing real estate for sale. In addition, the guide also printed feature articles and community notices of interest to those buying and selling real estate. Picket Fence claimed that it met Vermont's definition of a newspaper. Thus, according to Picket Fence, to deny its claim to the use tax exemption while allowing it to publish newspapers violated its rights both under the Equal Protection Clause and the First Amendment.

The Vermont Supreme Court held that the publication did not meet the definition of a newspaper. Furthermore, there was no Equal Protection violation because the state's distinction between newspapers and other publications rested upon a legitimate interest in encouraging widespread, inexpensive distribution of the news. Finally, the Court held that since the determination of what constituted a newspaper in Vermont was not content-based, there was no First Amendment free speech violation. [*In re* Picket Fence Preview, 795 A.2d 1242 (Vermont, Mar. 22, 2002)]

Chapter 3

Taxable Persons

This chapter reviews the general characteristics of sales and use tax, who must collect the tax, who must pay it, and the general categories of exemptions common to most states. Every state with a sales tax also has a complementary use tax. The use tax is usually assessed on the storage, use, or consumption of tangible personal property and selected services sold at retail, and upon which no sales tax was previously paid. The purported goal of the use tax is to create a "level playing field" between in-state and out-of-state sellers. Absent a use tax, a purchaser could avoid the local sales tax by buying items from out-of-state sellers who have no obligation to collect the local sales tax. With a use tax in place, the purchaser is obligated to remit to the state an amount equal to the unpaid sales tax.

Who Bears the Tax?

Q 3:3 Which activities of an out-of-state vendor would create a duty to collect state taxes?

Quill v. North Dakota makes it clear that mail-order sales alone will not create nexus for an out-of-state seller. There must be some sort of physical presence. Because physical presence can only come through the presence of either people or property in the state, one is left with two questions: First, what kinds of activities in a state can people (employees, contractors, and third parties) perform before that activity constitutes more than the "slightest physical presence" determined for nexus? Second, how much property can be stored, used, or distributed in a state and for how long before that activity triggers nexus? States vary in their treatment of these questions, however, most apply their jurisdictional authority to the maximum extent permitted under the law.

People. [John C. Healy & Michael S. Schadewald, 2003 Multistate Corporate Tax Guide (Aspen Publishers 2003)] Employees, independent contractors, and third parties can all create sufficient physical presence to trigger nexus. An employee consistently and regularly working in a state (even if the employee's activities are unrelated to sales or marketing) will create nexus in every state. If an independent contractor, rather than an employee, is consistently and regularly working in a state performing the same activities as an employee, nexus is almost guaranteed. The disagreements between taxpayers and tax administrators over an employee's or contractor's presence in a state generally revolve around occasional trips into the state. Some perennial problem areas include deliveries, licensing software, installation, maintenance and repair, and attendance at trade shows.

Does an out-of-state retailer create nexus when it makes deliveries into another state in its own trucks? In *Miller Bros. v. Maryland* [347 U.S. 340 (1954)], the U.S. Supreme Court said no. Miller Brothers, a Delaware retailer, sold only to customers at its store in Wilmington. It did not take orders by mail or telephone. However, it did deliver goods, purchased by Maryland residents at its Wilmington store, by common carrier and in its own trucks. Maryland claimed that Miller Brothers was obligated to collect the state's use tax because (1) its advertising in Delaware newspapers and radio stations reached Maryland residents; (2) it mailed sales circulars to former customers, including customers in Maryland; and (3) it delivered purchases into Maryland by both common carrier and in its own trucks.

The U.S. Supreme Court held that the contacts between Miller Brothers and Maryland were insufficient to create nexus for sales and use tax. In an oft quoted sentence, Justice Jackson wrote, "Due process requires some definite link, some minimum connection, between a state and the person, property or transaction it seeks to tax." The occasional deliveries of goods in the seller's own trucks were not enough. "Here was no invasion or exploitation of the consumer market in Maryland. On the contrary, these sales resulted from purchasers traveling from Maryland to Delaware . . . " [Miller Bros. v. Maryland, 347 U.S. 340, 344–45 (1954)] In *Quill v. North Dakota* [504 U.S. 298 (1992)], the Supreme Court ruled that when the exploitation of a state's market is consistent and continuous, the "minimum contact" test of due process is satisfied and the out-of-state seller may have created nexus. As a consequence, more recent cases somewhat similar to *Miller Brothers* have gone against the taxpayer. For example, when a Missouri furniture store made more than 900 deliveries into Illinois over a nine-month period, "substantial nexus" created a filing obligation for the taxpayer. [Brown's Furniture, Inc. v. Wagner, 665 N.E.2d 795 (Ill.), *cert denied*, 519 U.S. 866 (1996)]

Thirty-nine states and the District of Columbia take the position that in-state delivery in the company's own vehicles creates nexus. The states include Arizona, Arkansas, California, Colorado, Connecticut, Georgia, Hawaii, Idaho, Indiana, Iowa, Kansas, Kentucky, Louisiana, Maine, Maryland, Michigan, Minnesota, Mississippi, Missouri, Nebraska, Nevada, New Jersey, New Mexico, North Carolina, North Dakota, Ohio, Oklahoma, Pennsylvania, Rhode Island, South Carolina, South Dakota, Tennessee, Texas, Utah, Vermont, Virginia, West Virginia, Wisconsin, and Wyoming. While most of the states reported that only one or two deliveries were sufficient to create a filing obligation, California set the threshold at two deliveries a month, and Virginia at 12 deliveries annually, and Idaho, Indiana, Tennessee, and Utah reported only that "regular" or "consistent" deliveries would create nexus.

Thirty-two states and the District of Columbia indicated that the licensing of software (if not *de minimis* as in *Quill*) creates nexus for sales and use tax. The states include Alabama, Arizona, Arkansas, Connecticut, Georgia, Hawaii, Idaho, Iowa, Kansas, Louisiana, Maine, Maryland, Michigan, Mississippi, Nebraska, New Mexico, North Carolina, North Dakota, Oklahoma, Pennsylvania, Rhode Island, South Carolina, South Dakota, Tennessee, Texas, Utah, Vermont, Virginia, Washington, West Virginia, Wisconsin, and Wyoming.

Thirty-six states and the District of Columbia claim that installation or maintenance of in-state property by an independent third party arranged by the out-of-state seller will create nexus for sales and use tax purposes. The states include Alabama, Arizona, Arkansas, California, Colorado, Connecticut, Georgia, Hawaii, Idaho, Iowa, Kansas, Kentucky, Louisiana, Maine, Maryland, Michigan, Minnesota, Mississippi, Nebraska, New Jersey, New Mexico, North Carolina, North Dakota, Ohio, Oklahoma, Pennsylvania, Rhode Island, South Carolina, South Dakota, Tennessee, Texas, Utah, Vermont, Washington, Wisconsin, and Wyoming.

The Multistate Tax Commission in Bulletin 95-1 asserts that an out-of-state computer retailer will create nexus in a state for sales and use tax when it contracts with an unrelated third party to perform repairs. The following 28 states and the District of Columbia have either adopted Bulletin 95-1 or maintain the same position: Alabama, Arizona, Arkansas, Colorado, Connecticut, Georgia, Idaho, Kansas, Louisiana, Maryland, Michigan, Minnesota, Nebraska, New Jersey, New Mexico, North Carolina, North Dakota, Ohio, Oklahoma, Pennsylvania, Rhode Island, South Carolina, South Dakota, Texas, Utah, Vermont, Washington, and Wyoming.

Whether attending an annual trade show created nexus for sales and use tax was addressed by the Florida Supreme Court in *Department of Revenue v. Share International, Inc.* [676 So. 2d 1362 (Fla. 1996), *cert. denied,* 65 U.S.L.W. 3465 (Jan. 6, 1997)]. Share International executives attended an annual three-day seminar in Florida where the company displayed and sold its products. The company collected and remitted sales tax on the trade-show sales but did not collect tax on its mail-order sales during the rest of the year. The Florida Department of Revenue argued that the attendance and sales at the annual trade show constituted "substantial nexus" and demanded that Share collect and remit sales tax on its mail-order sales. The Florida Supreme Court disagreed with the state, holding that Share's presence at the trade show did not constitute "substantial nexus." Recently, a few states have passed legislation providing that attendance at trade shows would not create a sales and use tax collection obligation. California, for example, provides that if an out-of-state retailer's participation and sales at trade shows or conventions do not exceed 15 days (formerly, 7 days) and $100,000 *net* income (formerly, $10,000 *gross* income), the retailer need not collect tax on its mail-order sales. [CRTC §6203] In contrast, 15 states assert that the attendance by a sales representative at a one- to two-day trade show is sufficient to create a sales and use tax obligation. The states include Alabama, Colorado, Connecticut, Idaho, Kansas, Louisiana, New Jersey, New Mexico, North Dakota, Oklahoma, Pennsylvania, Tennessee, Texas, Washington, and Wisconsin.

State decisions over whether occasional in-state visits to customers create nexus for sales and use tax vary dramatically and unfortunately offer little guidance to the tax practitioner. For example, 11 visits amounting to a little more than 40 hours to install card readers were deemed too isolated and sporadic to create nexus in Kansas [*In re* Appeal of Intercard, Inc., 14 P.3d 1111 (Kan. 2000)], but 41 visits over three years was enough to create nexus in New York. [Orvis Co. v. Tax Appeals Tribunal, 86 N.Y.2d 165, 654 N.E.2d 954, *cert. denied*, 516 U.S. 989 (1995)]

Property. [John C. Healy & Michael S. Schadewald, 2003 Multistate Corporate Tax Guide (Aspen Publishers 2003)] In years past, the question of how much property can be stored, used, or consumed in a state and for how long before that activity triggers nexus varied significantly from state to state. Now, most states hold that the storage, use, or consumption of any property in the state will most likely create nexus, in addition to being a taxable event. Generally, the only exceptions are for those items that qualify as immaterial or *de minimis* in those states that provide exemptions for temporary storage of inventory or other tangible personal property.

Inventory storage becomes more problematic when the items being stored are catalogs. The key question here is whether an out-of-state retailer creates nexus when the only activity in a state is the printing and distribution of its catalogs. While some states provide exemptions from sales and use tax for temporary storage, 23 states report that using an in-state printer to produce and store printed materials creates nexus for sales and use tax. The states included Alabama, Arizona, California, Colorado, Georgia, Hawaii, Idaho, Maine, Maryland, Michigan, Mississippi, Nebraska, New Jersey, New Mexico, North Carolina, North Dakota, Oklahoma, Rhode Island, South Dakota, Texas, Vermont, Virginia, and Wyoming.

Planning Point 3-2.1. Many states do offer temporary storage exemptions for items of tangible personal property that are intended to only be in the state for a short period of time and/or whose use may occur outside the state. For example, Wisconsin provides a temporary storage exemption for "printed advertising materials" if purchased for shipment and ultimate use outside the state. However, the state narrowly construes what qualifies as printed advertising materials, generally restricting it to printed words on paper. (Wis. § 77.54(25))

A purchasing agent entering the state to buy tangible personal property will create nexus in the District of Columbia and the following 19 states: Connecticut, Idaho, Illinois, Iowa, Louisiana, Maine, Nebraska, New Jersey, North Dakota, Oklahoma, Pennsylvania, South Dakota, Tennessee, Utah, Vermont, Virginia, Washington, West Virginia, and Wisconsin.

The growth in electronic commerce has raised additional questions related to the presence of property in a state. For example, if an out-of-state seller owns or leases a server in a state, will that create nexus for sales and use tax? The question is particularly tough because a server, while small and inexpensive, can be significant in maintaining a market for an out-of-state retailer. The answer to the question often hinges on whether the server's presence is *de minimis* or more than the "slightest physical presence." A Tennessee Chancery Court has ruled that the leasing of servers in the state does not constitute substantial nexus for either sales or franchise taxes. [America Online Inc. v. Johnson, No. 97-3786-III (Tenn. Ch. Ct. March 13, 2001)] The case was appealed to the Tennessee Court of Appeals, who reversed and remanded the case back to the lower court. Specifically, the court of appeals found that the question of physical presence is fact-specific and the court record as presented was insufficiently developed. [America Online Inc. v. Johnson, No. M2001-00927-COA-R#-CV (Tenn. Ct. App. July 30, 2002)]

Q 3:4 Can a corporation be required to collect a state's sale and use taxes because of the activities of a subsidiary or affiliated company?

If a subsidiary or a corporate affiliate has an agency relationship with the out-of-state vendor, the vendor will probably have to collect and remit that state's sales and use tax. What is at issue is the nature of the subsidiary or affiliate's activities. In 1960 the U.S. Supreme Court held that independent contractors could create nexus for an out-of-state retailer. "The test," according to the Supreme Court, "is simply the nature and extent of the activities" in the state. Where there was "continuous local solicitation," with the independent contractors performing the same role and functions as sales employees, the out-of-state seller has nexus with the state. [Scripto v. Carson, 362 U.S. 207, 208 (1960)]

If a third party acts as an agent for an out-of-state seller, that agency relationship may create nexus for the seller. A series of cases involving school book club sales is illustrative: *Scholastic Book Clubs v. State Board of Equalization* [207 Cal. App. 2d 734 (1st Dist. 1989) (out-of-state book club is deemed to have nexus because teachers collected money from the schoolchildren)]; *Pledger v. Troll Book Clubs Inc* [871 S.W.2d 389 (Ark. 1994) (teachers are not agents for the out-of-state book seller)]; *Scholastic Book Clubs v. Michigan Department of Treasury* [567 N.W.2d 692 (Mich. Ct. App. 1997) (taxpayer does not have nexus because teachers, lacking the authority to bind Scholastic, were not agents of Scholastic)]; *In re Scholastic Book Clubs, Inc.* [920 P.2d 947 (Kan. 1996) (Kansas Supreme Court holds that Scholastic has nexus because there existed an agency relationship with the schoolteachers)]. The different conclusions reached by the courts indicate the importance of a state's specific interpretation of its laws on agency. Some of the decisions are worrisome because substantial nexus is being asserted in the absence of a formal contract or compensation with the third party. States trying to establish nexus through an affiliate, "alter ego," or subsidiary often rely on the reasoning set forth in these cases.

Planning Point 3-2.2. Many taxpayers encounter nexus difficulties when they have subsidiaries that sell substantially similar products as the in-state company. In addition, while allowing an in-state vendor to accept returned merchandise and process credits on behalf of a mail order or online related company may make good sense from an operational viewpoint, it frequently creates problems for the remote subsidiary by allowing the states to assert that an "agency" relationship exists between the remote subsidiary and the in-state vendor. In addition, the possession of the returned goods owned by the remote subsidiary in the state can create nexus for that company. Taxpayers need to carefully weigh the benefits for their customers against these adverse tax consequences when establishing these relationships.

Thirteen states and the District of Columbia have indicated that an agency relationship with an in-state affiliate or subsidiary will create nexus for the out-of-state taxpayer. The states are Alabama,

Arkansas, Georgia, Idaho, Indiana, Minnesota, North Carolina, North Dakota, Ohio, South Carolina, South Dakota, Tennessee, and Wyoming.

Absent an agency relationship, states have been routinely unsuccessful in arguing that an out-of-state seller's affiliate creates nexus for the out-of-state taxpayer. Some states have tried to argue that the affiliate had an agency relationship with the out-of-state vendor because the two shared the same business names, trademarks, and logos, engaged in cross advertising, or were in similar lines of business. For example, Bloomingdale's had different affiliated corporate entities conducting sales in Pennsylvania, one by in-state retail stores, the other by mail-order catalog. Pennsylvania argued that the mail-order company had nexus because its corporate affiliate's in-state stores sold many of the same goods, shared advertising campaigns, and on two occasions accepted merchandise returns of items purchased by catalog. The state Commonwealth Court found for the taxpayer and rejected the state's argument that nexus existed because of an agency relationship between the affiliated corporations. [Bloomingdale's By Mail, Ltd. v. Department of Rev., 567 A.2d 773 (Pa. Commw. Ct. 1989), *aff'd without opinion*, 591 A.2d 1047 (Pa. 1991). Similar conclusions were found in two cases with Saks Fifth Avenue. [SFA Folio Collections Inc. v. Bannon, 217 Conn. 220 (1990), 585 A.2d 666 (Conn. 1991); SFA Folio Collections Inc. v. Tracy, 652 N.E.2d 693 (Ohio 1995)] The Ohio case is of particular interest because the state attempted to use the income tax "unitary" doctrine to assert substantial nexus for sales tax.

Corporations have historically been treated as separate taxable entities. In the income tax arena, however, the creation of "combined" reporting or "unitary" filing has prompted states to apply the unitary concept to sales and use tax. The unitary theory proposes ignoring separate corporate identities in favor of combining the operational activities of any number of companies that are involved in the same business activity. [*See* James T. Collins & Robert M. Kozub, State and Local Taxation Answer Book ch. 10 (Panel Publishers 2000), for a detailed discussion of the unitary theory of taxation.] It is unusual to see the unitary approach being applied to sales and use tax. The different nexus standards between income tax and sales and use tax coupled with the physical presence test in *Quill* make it seem unlikely that the unitary concept can be successfully applied to sales and use tax nexus.

Planning Point 3-3. As the previous discussion demonstrates, the area of nexus is complex and fraught with problems for multistate businesses. Although the physical presence threshold is a good guideline to adhere to, businesses frequently get into nexus problems by failing to revisit activities and underlying assumptions. Taxpayers would be well advised to periodically and regularly challenge their nexus assumptions to determine whether changes in activities now require the filing of returns or cessation in the filing of returns. In addition, through proactive planning, taxpayers may be able to structure their selling and marketing efforts in a manner that minimizes their nexus-creating activities. For example, it may be advantageous to create a marketing and advertising company with limited nexus-creating activities to distribute sales literature as a means of minimizing use tax expense.

Example 3-2. Vendor A has an extensive sales force, with at least one employee located in every state. From the home office, the members of the sales force send direct-mail solicitations for a new catalog division. The profits of the catalog division are being reduced by the taxes that are owed on the cost of the catalogs and other promotional literature that is being shipped into each state. Because the catalog operation is a division of Vendor A, the division has nexus in each location that Vendor A has employees. Furthermore, the catalog operation is required to collect sales tax on its catalog sales in each state. By dropping the catalog assets into a separate corporation with no assets or employees outside the home office state, the division will restrict the use tax due on catalogs to the home state and a few states that have specially constructed statutes that are designed to capture the distribution of promotional-type items. In addition to the savings of tax on the catalogs themselves, the division would also not be required to collect sales tax on their sales, which could also provide a substantial competitive advantage for Vendor A in all the states.

Exemptions and Exclusions

Q 3:18 Which types of charitable organizations are exempt from sales and use taxation?

The type of charitable organization which can purchase exempt from sales and use tax varies among the states. In general, the organization must be classified as an exempt organization under Internal

Revenue Code (IRC or Code) § 501. The following table lists the types of charitable organizations that the states (and the District of Columbia) exempt, at least to some extent, from sales and use taxes. [Recall from the discussion in Chapter 1, Q 1:6, that Alaska, Delaware, Montana, New Hampshire, and Oregon do not impose sales and use tax, so they are not listed in this and other tables.]

State Exemptions for Section 501 Organizations

State	*Type of Section 501 Organization*
Alabama	No § 501 organizations are exempt
Arizona	See specific state requirements
Arkansas	No § 501 organizations are exempt (other specific groups exempted)
California	No § 501 organizations are exempt
Colorado	§ 501(c)(3)
Connecticut	§ 501(c)(3), § 501(c)(13)
District of Columbia	§ 501(c)(3) if the organization has an office in the District of Columbia
Florida	§ 501(c)(3), § 501(c)(4), § 501(c)(19)
Georgia	§ 501(c)(3), § 501(c)(4), § 501(c)(19) (other specific groups exempted)
Hawaii	§ 501(c)(3)
Idaho	No § 501 organizations are exempt
Illinois	§ 501(c)(3), but must make an application to the Department of Revenue
Indiana	§ 501(c)(3), § 501(c)(4), § 501(c)(6), § 501(c)(8), § 501(c)(10), § 501(c)(19)
Iowa	No § 501 organizations are exempt (other specific groups exempted)
Kansas	Generally § 501(c)(3), but apply to the Department of Revenue
Kentucky	§ 501(c)(3)
Louisiana	No § 501 organizations are exempt
Maine	All § 501(c) groups exempted
Maryland	§ 501(c)(3), § 501(c)(13)
Massachusetts	§ 501(c)(3)
Michigan	§ 501(c)(3), § 501(c)(4)
Minnesota	§ 501(c)(3)
Mississippi	No § 501 organizations are exempt (other specific groups exempted)

State	*Type of Section 501 Organization*
Missouri	§ 501(c)(3), § 501(c)(4), § 501(c)(6), § 501(c)(10), § 501(c)(19)
Nebraska	§ 501(c)(3), but must also qualify under Nebraska Chapters 79 and 80
Nevada	§ 501(c)(3) and other specific Nevada statutory criteria
New Jersey	§ 501(c)(3)
New Mexico	No § 501 organizations are exempt
New York	§ 501(c)(3), § 501(c)(19), others might qualify
North Carolina	No § 501 organizations are exempt
North Dakota	No § 501 organizations are exempt
Ohio	§ 501(c)(3)
Oklahoma	Only those organizations specifically listed in the statutes
Pennsylvania	Must apply directly to the Pennsylvania Department of Revenue
Rhode Island	§ 501(c)(3)
South Carolina	§ 501(c)(3) (see Rev. Proc. 89-5)
South Dakota	§ 501(c)(3) and meet Admin. R. 64:06:01:38
Tennessee	§ 501(c)(3)
Texas	§ 501(c)(3), § 501(c)(4), § 501(c)(8), § 501(c)(10), § 501(c)(19)
Utah	§ 501(c)(3), and must apply to the Tax Commission for a benefit number
Vermont	§ 501(c)(3)
Virginia	Exemptions must be specifically granted by the General Assembly
Washington	Schools and other specified groups
West Virginia	§ 501(c)(3), § 501(c)(4)
Wisconsin	§ 501(c)(3)
Wyoming	§ 501(c)(3)

Key to Section 501 Organizations

§ 501(c)(3)	Organizations created and operated exclusively for religious, charitable, scientific, testing for public safety, literary, or educational purposes, or to foster national or international amateur sports, or the prevention of cruelty to children or animals

Key to Section 501 Organizations

§ 501(c)(4)	Civic leagues or organizations
§ 501(c)(6)	Business leagues, chambers of commerce, real estate boards, boards of trade, or professional football leagues not organized for profit
§ 501(c)(8)	Fraternal beneficial societies, orders, or associations operating under the lodge system or for the exclusive benefit of the members of a fraternity itself operating under the lodge system, and providing for the payment of life, sick, accident, or other benefits to the members of such society, order, or association or their dependents
§ 501(c)(10)	Domestic fraternal societies, orders, or associations, operating under the lodge system, the net earnings of which are devoted exclusively to religious, charitable, scientific, literary, educational, and fraternal purposes, and that do not provide for the payment of life, sick, accident, or other benefits
§ 501(c)(13)	Cemetery companies owned and operated exclusively for the benefit of their members or that are not operated for profit
§ 501(c)(19)	A post or organization of past or present members of the Armed Forces of the United States, or any auxiliary unit or society of, or a trust or foundation for, any such post or organization, organized in the United States or any of its possessions, at least 75% of the members of which are past or present members of the Armed Forces of the United States

Q 3:23 What are the requirements of a valid resale certificate?

A few states do not require a specific resale certificate and will accept a written statement so long as the written statement contains all the components of a certificate. For example, Colorado requires only that a seller have the purchaser's resale number on file. No other documentation is necessary. Most states, however, require specific documentation in the form of certificates. Virginia, for example, is more typical in requiring specialized exemption certificates for manufacturers, construction contractors, farmers, non-profit organizations, out-of-state dealers, and governmental agencies. In addition, Virginia has held that a certificate that "is incomplete, invalid, infirm or inconsistent on its face is never acceptable." [Ruling of the Tax Comm'r, No. 02-9, (Jan. 22, 2002); Va. Code § 58.1-623.]

As with other exemption certificates, state statutes or regulations usually detail the information needed on resale certificates. Generally, they must include the date, purchaser's name, address, license or seller's permit number, brief description of the goods being purchased justifying nontaxable treatment, and a signature. In addition, many states require that the seller acquire the resale certificate in good faith at the time of sale. One of the more interesting features of the Streamlined Sales Tax Project (SSTP) would drop the good faith requirement for vendors opting to collect tax under its auspices. This should simplify the process for vendors, as they would have a lower threshold for the adequacy of certificates. Whether the SSTP is implemented and whether states expand the relaxed standard to participating vendors remains to be seen; however, it seems clear that the states are acknowledging the exemption certificate burden placed upon vendors and are attempting to do something to improve the situation. In many states, resale certificates acquired weeks or months after the sale may be insufficient and convert an otherwise nontaxable transaction into a taxable one.

Planning Point 3-24. Vendors must be aware that exemption and resale certificates must be valid in order to remove from the vendor the liability for collecting the sales tax. If either certificate is not valid, the vendor has the responsibility to collect the tax, and failure to do so will expose the vendor to paying the tax, penalties, and interest upon audit. Vendors should also pay close attention to the differences in required information between resale and exemption certificates. For example, Virginia's requirements for electronic *resale* certificates are less demanding than its requirements for an electronic *exemption* certificate. [*See* Va. Pub. Doc. 0091, (May 19, 2000).]

Q 3:24 How long are exemption and resale certificates valid?

It depends upon the type of certificate. Blanket certificates, which often cover volume purchases, generally have no expiration date.

Specific sale certificates generally are more limited in scope and time. Each state has different requirements for renewing exemption and resale certificates. The following table lists these periods for the 45 states that impose sales and use tax and the District of Columbia.

Exemption and Resale Certificates' Validity Period

State	*Period*
Alabama	Generally, valid until revoked; some types expire in 12 or 36 months
Arizona	Purchaser applies the expiration date
Arkansas	No specific form required; customer's claim of certification must be documented
California	Generally, valid until revoked
Colorado	Generally, valid until revoked; contractor certificates issued for length of job
Connecticut	Generally, valid for 3 years; charitable exemption certificates are renewed annually
District of Columbia	Generally, valid until revoked
Florida	Generally, valid until revoked; exemption certificates expire in 5 years
Georgia	Generally, valid until revoked
Hawaii	Generally, valid until revoked or a material change in business activity
Idaho	No expiration date
Illinois	Generally, valid until revoked
Indiana	Generally, valid until revoked
Iowa	Generally, valid until revoked
Kansas	Generally, valid until revoked
Kentucky	Generally, valid until revoked
Louisiana	Generally, valid until revoked
Maine	Generally, valid until revoked
Maryland	Resale certificates are valid until revoked; 5 years for § 501(c)(3) entities
Massachusetts	Generally, valid until revoked
Michigan	Generally, 4 years
Minnesota	Generally, valid until revoked
Mississippi	Generally, valid until revoked
Missouri	5 years
Nebraska	3 years

State	Period
Nevada	Generally, valid until revoked; 5 years for § 501(c)(3) entities
New Jersey	Generally, valid until revoked
New Mexico	Valid until 12/31/04
New York	Generally, valid until revoked
North Carolina	Generally, valid until revoked or change in ownership
North Dakota	Exempt certificates indefinite; resale certificates, 1 year
Ohio	Generally, valid until revoked
Oklahoma	3 years
Pennsylvania	Generally, valid until revoked; blanket certificates, 5 years; § 501(c)(3) entities, 3 years
Rhode Island	Generally, valid until revoked
South Carolina	Generally, valid until revoked
South Dakota	Generally, valid until revoked
Tennessee	Generally, valid until revoked
Texas	Generally, valid until revoked
Utah	Generally, valid until revoked
Vermont	Generally, valid until revoked
Virginia	Generally, valid until revoked
Washington	4 years
West Virginia	Generally, valid until revoked
Wisconsin	Generally, valid until revoked
Wyoming	3 years or length of contract

Planning Point 3-25. Sellers making exempt sales should regularly refresh their exemption certificates, especially if they make regular sales to exempt entities or dealers for resale. This can make an excellent fill-in project for personnel who have seasonal work or for student interns.

Planning Point 3-26. Although each state has its own specific resale or exempt purchase certificate form, the Multistate Tax Commission (MTC) has developed a multijurisdictional exemption certificate form that can be used for a variety of exempt sales in most jurisdictions. Although many states impose limitations on the use of the MTC Uniform Sales and Use Tax Certificate—Multijurisdiction, the following states allow its use under varying conditions: Alabama, Arkansas, Arizona, California, Colorado, Connecticut, District of Columbia, Florida, Georgia, Hawaii, Idaho, Illinois, Iowa, Kansas, Kentucky, Maine, Maryland, Michigan, Minnesota, Missouri, Nebraska, Nevada, New Jersey, New Mexico, North Carolina, North Dakota, Ohio, Oklahoma, Pennsylvania, Rhode Island, South Carolina, South Dakota, Tennessee, Texas, Utah, Vermont, Washington, and Wisconsin.

Q 3:25 Do vendors that make only sales for resale need a sales and use tax number?

It varies by state. In most states and in the District of Columbia, vendors are required to have a sales and use tax number and satisfy the filing requirements. These states include Arkansas, California, Colorado, Connecticut, Florida, Georgia, Hawaii, Indiana, Iowa, Kentucky, Louisiana, Maine, Maryland, Massachusetts, Michigan (except for industrial and agricultural processors), Minnesota, Mississippi, Nevada, New Mexico, New York, North Carolina, North Dakota, Oklahoma, South Carolina, South Dakota, Tennessee, Texas, Utah, Washington, West Virginia, Wisconsin, and Wyoming.

Vendors are not required to have a sales and use tax number or satisfy the filing requirements in Alabama, Arizona, Idaho, Illinois, Iowa, Kansas, Minnesota, Missouri, Nebraska, New Jersey, Ohio, Pennsylvania, Rhode Island, Vermont, and Virginia.

Q 3:26 Can a vendor in one state use a resale certificate issued in another state to make a tax-free sale?

The majority of the states and the District of Columbia do not permit the use of another state's resale certificate to make a tax-free purchase. States prohibiting the use of another state's certificate include Arkansas, Colorado, Florida, Georgia, Hawaii, Idaho, Illinois, Indiana, Kansas, Kentucky, Louisiana, Maine, Michigan, Mississippi, Nebraska, Nevada, New Mexico, North Carolina, North Dakota, Ohio, Oklahoma, Pennsylvania, Rhode Island, South Carolina, South Dakota, Texas, Washington, and Wisconsin.

States that permit the use of another state's resale certificate to make tax-free purchases include Alabama (all states), Arizona (all states), California (only if a document contains the required elements as listed in Reg. § 1668), Connecticut (all states), Georgia (all states), Iowa (if another state's certificate meets the Iowa standards), Massachusetts, Minnesota (any state that meets the Minnesota requirements), Missouri (all states), New Jersey (only for drop-shipments for resale), New York (all states), Tennessee (all states), Utah, Vermont (if another state's certificate meets the Vermont standards), Virginia (all states), West Virginia (if another state's certificate meets the West Virginia standards), and Wyoming.

The majority of the states as well as the District of Columbia will also accept the Multistate Tax Commission's (MTC) Uniform Sales and Use Tax Certificate—Multijurisdiction in lieu of that state's sale for resale certificate. These states are Alabama, Arizona, California, Colorado, Georgia, Hawaii, Idaho, Indiana, Iowa, Kansas, Kentucky, Maine, Maryland (if the state has a Maryland registration number), Michigan, Minnesota, Missouri, Nebraska, Nevada, New Jersey, New Mexico, North Dakota, Ohio, Oklahoma, Pennsylvania, South Carolina, South Dakota, Tennessee, Texas, Utah, Vermont, Virginia, and West Virginia.

The states that do not accept the MTC's Uniform Sales and Use Tax Certificate—Multijurisdiction include Arkansas, Florida, Illinois, Louisiana, Massachusetts, Mississippi, New York, North Carolina, Rhode Island, Washington, Wisconsin, and Wyoming.

Planning Point 3-27. The unwillingness of some states to accept another state's resale certificate creates serious compliance problems for sales involving drop-shipments. The most common drop-shipment transaction is structured as follows: a retailer in State A sells goods to a buyer in State B and has the goods drop-shipped from its manufacturer (also in State B) to the buyer. The retailer does not have nexus with nor is it registered to do business in State B. If an auditor for State B asks the manufacturer for the retailer's resale number, it can only offer State A's resale number. If the auditor refuses to honor a resale certificate from State A, how does the manufacturer avoid a sales tax assessment on its resale sales? In some states, like California and Wisconsin, the manufacturer must collect the tax from the customer, even though there is no contract of sale between the manufacturer and the retailer's customer. Depending upon the drop-shipment scenario multiple taxation and unanticipated assessments can be the result. Frequently the only viable solutions to this problem are either (1) acquiring a sales tax license or seller's permit from State B or (2) billing the tax as a cost recovery. Many states have special registration requirements for vendors that wish to voluntarily register to collect tax as a vendor accommodation or to avoid drop-shipment problems.

Chapter 4

Taxable Transactions

The majority of states tax the retail sale of tangible property and select services. Exemptions are specifically enumerated. (*See* Chapters 6 and 7 for specific inclusions and exclusions.) This chapter examines what constitutes a taxable sale and highlights some of the perennial problem transactions that are sometimes specifically included or excluded from the definition of a taxable sale.

Sales for Resale

Q 4:3 Are sales for resale subject to sales and use taxes?

Generally no. Resale sales are usually exempt from sales and use taxes because they are intermediate transactions; that is, they are sales to vendors who in turn will charge sales tax upon their retail sale to the final consumer. The resale exclusion, however, does not apply to all items purchased and transferred to the end user. A seller providing a service must pay sales tax on the items consumed in the course of providing the service. In fact, a vendor's purchase of tangible personal property may be taxable even where some of the property is transferred in a sale of services to the end consumer.

States generally rely on one of two tests in determining whether a sale is a potentially taxable retail sale or an exempt sale for resale. The "physical ingredient test" simply asks whether the raw material became part of the product being sold. If it has become an ingredient, integral, or component part of property that itself will be sold, then the purchase of the material will qualify as a sale for resale. The Louisiana Court of Appeals has nicely summarized the theory behind the physical ingredient test.

> The raw material becomes an integral part of the article to be sold at retail, the cost price or sales price of that raw material is theoretically incorporated into the sales price of the article, and the tax will be collected or paid when that article is later sold or used. The tax will be levied not upon the manufacturer, but upon the *retail purchaser, user, or consumer*, of the manufactured item. Conversely, when a thing or raw material . . . does not become an integral, beneficial part of the manufactured item, the manufacturer is the ultimate *retail purchaser, user, consumer,* and is obligated to pay the sales or use tax. (emphasis added by the court)

[McNamara v. UOP, Inc., 389 So. 2d 741, 747-748 (La. Ct. App. 1980)]

The primary purpose test would exempt raw material or property that becomes an ingredient part of property for sale at retail only if the main reason for purchasing the raw material was to incorporate it within the property being sold at retail. Thus, items purchased that serve a dual purpose or are used as catalysts or bonding agents may be taxable even if they remain part of the finished product. [Kaiser Steel Corp. v. State Board of Equalization, 593 P.2d 864 (1979)]

Naturally, courts have varied in their findings as to which standard, physical ingredient or primary purpose, is appropriate. For example, Washington's Supreme Court ruled that the State's Department of Revenue could not use the primary purpose test while Nevada's Supreme Court recently ruled that the primary purpose test was the appropriate standard in that state. [*See* Lone Star, Inc. v. Dep't of Rev., 647 P.2d 1013 (1982) and Nevada Tax Comm'n v. Nevada Cement Co., No. 33178 (Nev. Sup. Ct., Dec. 12, 2001).]

The following are examples of sales that illustrate the application of these rules.

Example 4-2. A store purchases shirts from a wholesaler to sell to its customers. The store does not pay sales tax to its wholesaler on the purchase of the shirts but collects the tax from its retail customers.

Example 4-3. A bank has purchased promotional items such as toasters or microwave ovens that will be given to depositors who open a new account with the bank. The bank is not in the business of selling such items and has purchased these items for its own use, i.e., promotion of new accounts. Because the bank has not purchased these items for resale, they are subject to sales tax at the time the bank buys them.

Example 4-4. A vendor purchases catalogs and distributes them to potential customers below its cost for a minimal charge. Some states might allow the vendor to purchase the catalogs for resale if the vendor charges sales tax on the minimal charge it makes to its customers. Other states might insist on some additional use tax on the difference between the cost of the catalogs and the taxable sales price to the customers. Finally, some states may take the position that the vendor is subject to tax upon its purchase of the catalogs because the items are not really for resale but rather for the vendor's own use, i.e., promotion.

Example 4-5. A book publisher purchases leather for making bookbindings for books that it sells directly to the public at retail. Because the leather has become a physical component part of the books sold at retail, the purchase of the leather qualifies as a resale exclusion and is not subject to tax.

Example 4-6. A shoe repairman purchases leather to be used for resoling shoes. In some states, the purchase of the leather is not a purchase for resale, even though the leather will be transferred to the customer in connection with the performance of the service, because the service is not taxable. The repairman is treated as the consumer. In other states, the purchase is not taxable, because the repairman is not considered the ultimate consumer or the material is considered incidental to the repair. [*See* Chapter 6.]

Example 4-7. A dentist purchases gold to be used as fillings and crowns. The purchase by the dentist is not for resale, even though the gold is transferred to the patient in the performance of the dentist's service.

Planning Point 4-2. The best way for a seller to document that a sale is a nontaxable qualifying resale is to acquire a resale certificate from the purchaser. In fact, it is a requirement in most states. According to the Multistate Tax Commission, "whenever a vendor receives and accepts in good faith from a purchaser a resale or other exemption certificate . . . authorized by the appropriate State . . . the vendor shall be relieved of liability for a sales or use tax with respect to the transaction." It should be noted that the seller must take the resale certificate in "good faith." The "good faith" requirement means that the vendor has no reason to believe that the purchaser is using the item for any reason other than for resale. Vendors that have or should have reason to believe that an item is not being resold or used in an exempt manner are required to bill the tax to their customer despite the receipt of a resale or other exemption certificate. In a Kentucky case, a janitor supply store's "good faith" was severely questioned. The court stated, "It is ludicrous that the appellee could have received in good faith the resale certificate from a funeral home which purchased a weed killer." [Dep't of Rev. v. Warren Chem. & Janitor Supply Co., 562 S.W.2d 644, 646 (Ky. Ct. App. 1977)]

Planning Point 4-3. Although a resale or other exemption certificate is the most appropriate proof that an exempt sale has taken place, some states allow vendors to submit other proof of exemption in lieu of a certificate. For example, to establish that a sale for resale has occurred, vendors may submit a purchase order that contains the necessary information for exemption or a contract that provides the required data.

Planning Point 4-4. Generally, the best time to obtain a resale or other exemption certificate is before the sale is made. At this point in the transaction, the taxpayer has the most control over the billing to the customer and can charge tax if the customer does not provide adequate proof of exemption. Waiting until after the sale has been completed to secure the exemption certificate places the seller at risk of never receiving the documentation necessary to shield the seller from future exposure. New York State has a very strict requirement that to be considered valid, the exemption certificate must be obtained within 60 days of the sale.

Casual or Occasional Sale

Q 4:21 What is the sales and use tax treatment of casual sales?

A majority of the states provide an exemption for casual, isolated, or occasional sales. Casual sales are not exempt in Colorado, Oklahoma, and Wyoming. The exemption is generally limited to sales by persons not regularly engaged in selling tangible personal property. Annual garage sales, for example, are commonly exempt as casual or occasional sales. Traditional retailers and vendors are usually not eligible for casual sale exemptions. However, exceptions do exist for auctions, liquidations, and bulk sales of an entire business. Court opinions have been mixed, but generally negative, as to whether the occasional sale exemption applies to the sale of an item dissimilar to that sold in the regular course of business. For example, would the sale of counters and shelving by a retail toy store that is in the midst of remodeling qualify as an occasional or casual sale? Usually not, but exceptions do exist. [Staley v. Missouri, 623 S.W.2d 246 (Mo. 1981)] Sales of licensed vehicles such as motor vehicles, trailers, airplanes, boats, and motorcycles are rarely exempt as a casual sale. In addition, most state registration processes require payment of the sales/use tax before titling. Therefore, it is very unusual for a licensed vehicle to escape taxation. Casual, isolated, or occasional sales are often limited in frequency and dollar amount by regulation.

Limitations on Casual, Occasional, or Isolated Sales

State	*Maximum Number of Casual Sales per Year*	*Dollar Limit on Casual Sales*
Alabama	Casual sales by persons not engaged in selling are generally exempt.	No $ Limit
Arizona	Casual sales by persons not engaged in selling are generally exempt.	No $ Limit
Arkansas	1	No $ Limit
California	2	No $ Limit
Colorado	No exemption for casual, occasional, or isolated sales.	
Connecticut	Must be infrequent.	No $ Limit

State	*Maximum Number of Casual Sales per Year*	*Dollar Limit on Casual Sales*
District of Columbia	Casual sales by persons not engaged in selling are generally exempt.	
Florida	2	No $ Limit
Georgia	Casual sales by persons not engaged in selling are generally exempt, as are 30-day business liquidations.	No $ Limit
Hawaii	Casual sales by persons not engaged in selling are generally exempt.	
Idaho	2	No $ Limit
Illinois	1	No $ Limit
Indiana	Casual sales by persons not engaged in selling are generally exempt.	
Iowa	2	No $ Limit
Kansas	1	No $ Limit
Kentucky	2	No $ Limit
Louisiana	Casual sales by persons not engaged in selling are generally exempt.	No $ Limit
Maine	Casual sales by persons not engaged in selling are generally exempt.	No $ Limit
Maryland	1	$1,000
Massachusetts	1	No $ Limit
Michigan	1	No $ Limit
Minnesota	Casual sales by persons not engaged in selling are generally exempt.	No $ Limit
Mississippi	Casual sales by persons not engaged in selling are generally exempt.	No $ Limit
Missouri	Casual sales by persons not engaged in selling are generally exempt.	$3,000

State	*Maximum Number of Casual Sales per Year*	*Dollar Limit on Casual Sales*
Nebraska	Casual sales by persons not engaged in selling are generally exempt.	No $ Limit
Nevada	2	No $ Limit
New Jersey	Casual sales by persons not engaged in selling are generally exempt.	No $ Limit
New Mexico	Casual sales by persons not engaged in selling are generally exempt.	No $ Limit
New York	3 (garage sales)	$600
North Carolina	No Limit	No $ Limit
North Dakota	Casual sales by persons not engaged in selling are generally exempt.	No $ Limit
Ohio	1 (non-business, non-permanent auctions)	No $ Limit
Oklahoma	No exemption for casual, occasional, or isolated sales.	
Pennsylvania	3	No $ Limit
Rhode Island	5 (Yard sales limited to one per year)	No $ Limit
South Carolina	Casual sales by persons not engaged in selling are generally exempt.	No $ Limit
South Dakota	Casual sales by persons not engaged in selling are generally exempt.	No $ Limit
Tennessee	Casual sales by persons not engaged in selling are generally exempt.	No $ Limit
Texas	2	No $ Limit
Utah	Casual sales by persons not engaged in selling are generally exempt.	No $ Limit
Vermont	Casual sales by persons not engaged in selling are generally exempt.	No $ Limit

State	*Maximum Number of Casual Sales per Year*	*Dollar Limit on Casual Sales*
Virginia	3	No $ Limit
Washington	Casual sales by persons not engaged in selling are generally exempt.	No $ Limit
West Virginia	Casual sales by persons not engaged in selling are generally exempt.	No $ Limit
Wisconsin	Casual sales by persons not engaged in selling are generally exempt.	No $ Limit
Wyoming	No exemption for casual, occasional, or isolated sales.	

Planning Point 4-11. Many states exempt casual or occasional sales such as garage sales, because the compliance costs exceed the tax revenue earned. However, despite an occasional victory, licensed vendors should note that most states do not exempt any tangible personal property sales by a registered vendor, including sales of equipment or assets used in a trade or business.

Withdrawals from Inventory

Q 4:24 What are the most common inventory withdrawals subject to use taxation?

The more common types of withdrawals include those for personal use, routine business use, the manufacture of self-constructed assets, research and experimentation, promotional items including samples, and donations to charity. Some examples follow:

Withdrawals for Personal Use

Example 4-9. Dan is the single proprietor of a small toy store in a local mall. The week before Christmas he withdraws some toys from his inventory as presents from Santa Claus for his own two children. Because Dan originally bought these items for resale and is now converting them to personal use, he must pay use tax on *his* cost of the toys withdrawn, not the fair market value.

Withdrawals for Routine Business Use

Example 4-10. An auto parts store purchases oil and other auto goods for resale. When the business's delivery truck needs an oil change, the store simply pulls a few cans from the oil purchased for resale. The store owes use tax when the oil is withdrawn and used in the oil change.

Example 4-11. A brewery allows its employees two free cases of its beer each month as a fringe benefit. Because the beer was brewed for resale, neither sales nor use tax was paid on malt, barley, grain, or other ingredients to manufacture the beer. The company owes use tax on the material cost of the beer given away to employees.

Withdrawals for Use in Producing Self-Constructed Assets

Example 4-12. Ace Machine & Tool Shop needs another drill press. After looking at a couple of presses, the company believes it can build its own press for less cost. Ace Machine manufactures a drill press, taking the steel and necessary parts from its own inventory. Ace owes use tax on the materials withdrawn from inventory. Some states exempt machinery purchased or self-constructed that is used in manufacturing. If Ace's drill press qualifies for the exemption, no use tax will be due, as long as the press is "used in manufacturing" under the applicable state statute.

Withdrawals for Research and Experimentation

Example 4-13. Hi-Tech Computer manufactures motherboards for personal computers. It routinely transfers small amounts of materials from inventory for use in research and experimentation (R&E). It also pulls boards from the production line for testing. The boards are usually destroyed either during or after testing. Absent a specific sales and use tax exemption for either R&E or testing, Hi-Tech will owe use tax on its inventory withdrawals.

Withdrawals of Samples and Promotional Items

There has been a great deal of litigation over the application of sales and use tax to samples and promotional items. Promotional consumer items can include free product samples, T-shirts, hats, sports clothing, coffee mugs, key chains, calendars, notepads, and can openers. Promotional business items are often product displays such as posters, racks, banners, signage, and other displays placed in retail outlets. Generally, these items are produced by third parties and may be drop-shipped directly to the company's distributors and retailers or to warehouses around the country for temporary storage.

The litigation over promotional items and samples has revolved around two key issues. First, do purchases of promotional items qualify for the resale exclusion as items purchased for resale? For example, the Milwaukee Brewers gave away baseball caps, jackets, and seat cushions to spectators who attended their games. The team argued that the items were purchased for resale, because they were available only to fans paying admission to the games. The court disagreed. [Wisconsin Dep't of Rev. v. Milwaukee Brewers, 111 Wis. 2d 571, 331 N.W.2d 383 (1983). *But see* Kansas City v. Director of Rev., No. SC82554 (Mo. Dec. 5, 2000), for a contrary holding.] An Ohio court, however, held that bonus items included upon the purchase of a certain quantity of goods were not subject to use tax, because the items were treated as a discount to the sales price. [Electrolert Inc. v. Joanne Limbach, Tax Comm'r of Ohio, No. 89-J-94 (Ohio Bd. of Tax App. Mar. 13, 1993); Virginia Dep't of Rev. in Ruling of the Comm'r, PD 94-14 (Jan. 13, 1994)] Toys packaged with fast-food purchases have also been held to be exempt from sales tax as a resale item. [Ariz. Rul. TPR 93-45; *In re* Petition of E-M Food Corp., DTA Nos. 809808, 809809, 809810, 809811 (N.Y. Div. of Tax App., Admin. Law Judge Unit Mar. 18, 1993)]

The second key issue with regard to promotional items is jurisdictional. If a third-party contractor manufactures promotional items and drop-ships them to distributors all over the United States, where is the taxable use? Is it in the state where the contractor is located? Is it in the state where the owner of the promotional items is located? Or is it in every state to which the items are drop-shipped? (The last question raises yet another. Does the distribution by the contractor of the promotional items create nexus for the retailer for whom the goods are being made?) The litigation on promotional items, particularly catalogs, seems unending. [For some examples, begin with D.H. Holmes v. McNamara, 486 U.S. 24 (1988); Sharper Image v. Michigan, No. 92-14443-CM (Ct. Cl. Feb. 28, 1994); May Dep't Stores v. Director of Rev., 748 S.W.2d 174 (Mo. 1988); Sharper Image v. Arizona, Div.

1, Dep't T, No. 1 CA-TX 97-0017 (Ariz. Ct. App. May 5, 1998); Service Merchandise v. Schwartzberg, No. 96CA1446 (Colo. Ct. App. Dec. 26, 1997).]

Planning Point 4-13.1. All taxpayers should have a use tax self-assessment procedure in place to capture any unpaid tax due on purchases from vendors that are not registered to collect sales tax on otherwise taxable transactions. For most businesses, use tax represents an area of significant exposure when audited. By initiating a simple procedure to self-assess tax on all purchases where the purchase order indicates that it is a taxable transaction and the vendor failed to bill tax, taxpayers can greatly reduce their audit exposure. In addition, when the overall audit deficiency is reduced, there is less chance of a penalty imposition in most states and lower interest charges when the audit is billed.

Withdrawals for Donation to Charitable Organizations

Generally, the donation of otherwise taxable property to a qualified charitable or not-for-profit organization is not a taxable transaction, because it is not a "sale" as that is defined for sales and use tax. There is no consideration being received by the donor. The donation itself is not usually a taxable event. There will be no sales or use tax due if the donor paid tax upon the original purchase of the property. It is the withdrawal from inventory of property purchased tax-free that triggers the use tax liability. Unless a state's statute specifically exempts from the use tax the contribution of inventory withdrawals to qualified charitable organizations, the donor must pay use tax at the time of withdrawal.

States that exempt donations of property include California (if to a California charity, otherwise taxable), Colorado, Connecticut, Hawaii, Illinois, Kentucky, Massachusetts, Michigan, Nevada (unless some promotional benefit is derived by the donor), New Mexico, New York, North Carolina, North Dakota, Ohio, Texas, Utah, Vermont, Virginia, West Virginia, Washington, Wisconsin, and the District of Columbia.

Some states will allow the donation tax-free treatment if other eligibility requirements are met. For example, California limits the exemption for donations to charitable organizations located in California. New York restricts the exemption to specific donors and to specific uses of the property. A New York manufacturer or processor is eligible for the use tax exemption only if the property donated is the same as that sold in the regular course of business and no prior use has been made of the donated property. Retailers, wholesalers, and others must pay tax on the donated property at the time it is purchased. [N.Y. Tax Law § 1115(1); 20 N.Y. Comp. Codes R. & Regs. 528.28]

The key question for donated property withdrawn from inventory is often one of who receives the tax. Is it the state where the property is withdrawn? Is it the state where the charity is located? Is it the state where title passes? Or is it the state where the goods were originally purchased? The majority of states hold that the state in which the items are withdrawn from inventory should receive the use tax due. The states in the majority are Alabama, Arizona, Arkansas, Florida, Georgia, Idaho, Illinois, Iowa, Kansas, Louisiana, Maine, Michigan, Minnesota, Mississippi, Missouri, Nebraska, New York, Pennsylvania, Rhode Island, South Carolina, South Dakota, Tennessee, and Wyoming. A few states—Maryland, New Jersey, and Oklahoma tax the goods in the state where the charity receives the property. Connecticut and Indiana look to the state where title passed.

Planning Point 4-14. Taxpayers wishing to avoid the use tax liability on donated property may want to consider donating the cash to the charitable organization in lieu of the property. The charitable entity could then purchase the item from the taxpayer without payment of tax. Care should be exercised in structuring the donation because a donation that is contingent upon the purchase of inventory from the taxpayer is not a valid charitable contribution and the contribution deduction may be forfeited.

Exemptions

Q 4:25 Do states provide a sales and use tax exemption for machinery used in manufacturing and other industrial use?

Yes. Many states provide either that machinery and equipment used in manufacturing are exempt from sales tax or that the tax is assessed at a reduced rate. Most of the exemptions were passed as an incentive for manufacturers to relocate, expand, or remain within the state. The machinery purchases often must meet additional requirements such as "direct and exclusive" use in manufacturing to be eligible for the exemption or reduced rate. It is not unusual to find agricultural or farm states with exemptions for agricultural machinery and equipment.

Planning Point 4-15. In addition to providing exemptions for machinery and equipment used in the manufacturing process, many states also provide exemptions for supplies that are consumed or destroyed, or that lose their identity in the manufacturing process. States also provide exemptions for machinery and equipment used for pollution abatement or pollution control. The majority of states provide exemptions for packaging equipment and materials used for packaging and shipping products to the final consumer. These exemptions vary from state to state.

Three states impose sales and use tax at a reduced rate on production machinery and equipment. Two states provide refunds for capital equipment acquired for new or expanding industries. A limited number of states—Hawaii, Louisiana, Nebraska, Nevada, New Mexico, South Dakota, Washington, and Wyoming—as well as the District of Columbia—tax production machinery at the standard rate. [*See* Chapter 6, Machinery and Equipment, for detailed treatment.]

One of the key areas of disagreement between tax professionals and administrators is in defining the scope of manufacturing for purposes of the sales and use tax exemption. For example, is a dairy plant that processes milk in manufacturing? What about meat-packing plants, plants canning peaches, printing plants, ready-mix concrete plants, or plants processing scrap? Many state statutes have incorporated language used by the U.S. Supreme Court in a 1956 case. "Manufacturing implies a change. . . . There must be a transformation; a new and different article must emerge, having a distinctive name, character, or use." [East Tex. Motor Freight Lines v. Frozen Foods Express, 351 U.S. 49 (1956)] In addition, state statutes often require that the machinery cost in excess of a certain amount, be used in the state, and act upon or have a positive direct effect on the raw material being manufactured. Questions and litigation continue to arise over activities such as shipping and receiving, conveyor equipment, packaging, storage, waste removal, research and development, testing and quality control, mandatory safety equipment, repair and maintenance, and plant heating, lighting, and cooling.

Planning Point 4-16. Many states utilize the Standard Industrial Classification (SIC) Codes as a starting point to determine whether a taxpayer is a manufacturer. In most states, there is a requirement that the manufacturing process be one that is "popularly regarded" as manufacturing. Taxpayers falling outside the standard classification as a manufacturer may still qualify if they can demonstrate that they sufficiently transform tangible personal property. However, qualifying outside the statutes usually requires an appeal to the state department of revenue.

Planning Point 4-16.1. A common misconception is that qualifying as a manufacturer makes all an entity's purchases tax exempt. This is hardly the case. Many manufacturers will still have substantial sales and use tax expense because of a state's limitations on its definition of manufacturing and related exemptions. Typically, taxable items include: administrative supplies, advertising, marketing and promotional materials, research and development equipment and supplies (unless state defines manufacturing to include research and development), maintenance equipment and tools, and stock room equipment, just to name a few of the more commonly taxable items.

Q 4:29 Is agricultural machinery exempt from state sales and use taxes?

Usually. The majority of states exempt agricultural machinery from sales and use tax if the purchaser is engaged in farming, agriculture, horticulture, or floriculture. [*See* Chapter 6.] Five states impose a lower sales and use tax rate: Alabama (1.5 percent), Florida (2.5 percent), Mississippi (1 percent or 3 percent), North Carolina (1 percent with $80 maximum tax per item), and North Dakota (3 percent on new equipment only). California, Hawaii, Nevada, New Mexico, Wyoming, and the District of Columbia have no exemption for agricultural machinery. As with manufacturing machinery, states may impose additional direct-use, exclusive-use, or predominant-use requirements to qualify for exemption. Sales of feed, seed, and fertilizer used in food production are often considered exempt.

Chapter 5

Interstate and Extraterritorial Transactions

States can constitutionally tax only retail sales occurring within their borders. As a consequence, interstate commerce clause considerations have prompted states to exempt from sales tax sales shipped out-of-state. This fact, and the constitutional implications surrounding it, raises questions about the taxing of property or services purchased in one state and used in another, the interstate sales taxation of telecommunications, and more generally, the impact of the Internet and electronic commerce on the taxing powers of state governments. It is to these and related interstate tax questions we turn in this chapter.

Taxing Local Activity

Q 5:4 Can a seller refute the state's presumption of where a sale occurs?

The following 20 states and the District of Columbia provide sellers a rebuttable presumption regarding a sale's location: Colorado, Georgia, Idaho, Iowa, Maryland, Massachusetts, Michigan, Minnesota, Missouri, New Mexico, New York, North Dakota, Ohio, South Carolina, Tennessee, Texas, Vermont, West Virginia, Wisconsin, and Wyoming.

Taxability of Property Purchased or Leased in One State and Used in Another

Q 5:8 Has the interpretation of the Interstate Commerce Clause restrictions on state taxation remained consistent over time?

No. One of the goals of those drafting the United States Constitution was to prohibit states from erecting barriers to interstate trade. For example, New Jersey used to tax goods being transported from New York across New Jersey to Philadelphia. Other states established tariffs to keep out goods from other states competing with their own manufacturers. Thus, for many years the Commerce Clause was interpreted as creating a sort of national "free-trade" zone. Under this interpretation, the focus was on distinguishing between activities that were purely local in nature from those activities that were national. To that end, the key questions addressed by the courts for tax purposes included such things as determining whether the tax was applied to an activity either before or after it entered the stream of interstate commerce; whether the activity taxed was purely local in nature; and whether the tax directly or indirectly had an impact on interstate commerce. A good example of state taxing efforts under this approach is the attempt to find in a local or intrastate activity a taxable moment when an item was no longer in the stream of interstate commerce. For example, Colorado assessed use tax on airplanes purchased outside the state but brought into Colorado for use by a commercial airline. The court held that "there was, therefore, a time, however short, during which these aircraft had ceased to be goods shipped in interstate commerce and had not yet been placed in interstate commercial use. This moment was the 'taxable moment' as defined by the U.S. Supreme Court.'' [Aspen Airways, Inc. v. Heckers, 499 P.2d 636 (Colo. Ct. App. 1972). For similar rulings on the ''taxable moment'' in other states, see Flying Tiger Line, Inc. v. State Bd. of Equalization, 320 P.2d 552 (Cal. 1958); *In re* Protest of Woods Corp., 531 P.2d 1381 (Okla. 1975); Sundstrand Corp. v. Department of Revenue, 339 N.E.2d 351 (Ill. 1975).]

Today, state revenue departments and courts need not search for an intrastate taxable moment or a local incident distinct from interstate commerce in order to uphold a tax under the Commerce Clause. Since the U.S. Supreme Court decision in *Complete Auto Transit v. Brady* [430 U.S. 274 (1977)], all a tax must do to pass constitutional muster under the Commerce Clause is to (1) be applied to an activity with a substantial nexus with the taxing state; (2) be fairly apportioned; (3) not discriminate against interstate commerce; and (4) be fairly related to the services provided by the state. Despite the less stringent tests of *Complete Auto Transit*, taxpayers and practitioners should not assume that all states have adopted those tests. For example, the Arkansas Supreme Court recently ruled that natural gas shipped in interstate commerce and consumed in Arkansas was not taxable in the state because it had not ''come-to-rest'' before being consumed. Because the ''come-to-rest'' test was codified in the Arkansas code (Ark. Code Ann. § 26-35-106(b)), the court declined to replace it with the *Complete Auto Transit* tests. [Mississippi River Transp. Corp. Inc. v. Weiss, No. 99-2762 (Ark. Sup. Ct. Feb. 7, 2002)]

Interstate Sales Taxation of Telecommunications Services

Q 5:11 Is state taxation of telecommunications services constitutional?

Yes. The U.S. Supreme Court has upheld the constitutionality of a tax on the gross charges for interstate telecommunications services in Illinois. The Court held that such a tax would be constitutional so long as it met two of three tests: the calls either originated, terminated, or were billed to an Illinois address. [Goldberg v. Sweet, 488 U.S. 252 (1989)] The Court noted that despite the fact that the call might travel through several states, only one state would be able to meet two of the three tests. This fact, coupled with the credit offered by Illinois against any other state taxing the same transaction, prompted the Court to hold that the tax did not discriminate against interstate commerce.

Despite the landmark implications of the *Goldberg* two-out-of-three test for state and local taxation, the federal Mobile Telecommunications Sourcing Act [Pub. L. No. 106-252 (July 28, 2000)(effective Aug. 1, 2002)] makes application of *Goldberg* largely irrelevant with respect to mobile communications. The Act is designed to simplify the sales and use tax compliance problems associated with sourcing cell phone use. In brief, the federal Act supersedes the *Goldberg* decision and sources cell phone calls to a customer's "primary place of business." The new law means that cell phone providers will no longer have to source each phone call for sales and use tax purposes. Instead, the customers will be charged the sales tax applicable to their "primary place of use" no matter where the customer's calls are made or received. A customer's "primary place of use" will be either "the residential street address," or "the primary business street address," or "the licensed service area of the home service provider."

Forty-nine states and the District of Columbia have adopted the Mobile Telecommunications Sourcing Act. Montana's legislature passed conforming legislation only to see it vetoed by Governor Judy Martz (R). Since Montana does not currently have a sales tax or impose any other tax on mobile telecommunications, Governor Martz vetoed the bill because it amounted to a tax increase.

Q 5:12 Which states impose a sales tax on telecommunications services?

Forty-two states and the District of Columbia impose either a sales or an excise tax on telecommunications services. Georgia (4 percent) and the District of Columbia (5.75 percent) tax only local exchange service. Fifteen states tax only intrastate calls: Alabama (6 percent), Arizona (5.6 percent), California (0.72 percent), Colorado (2.9 percent), Indiana (6 percent), Iowa (5 percent), Kentucky (6 percent), Maine (5 percent), Missouri (4.225 percent), Nebraska (5.5 percent; 5 percent effective Oct. 1, 2003), New York (4 percent), North Dakota (5 percent), South Dakota (4 percent), Utah (5.75 percent), and Wyoming (4 percent).

Twenty states tax both intrastate and interstate phone services at the same rate. These states include Arkansas (5.125 percent), Connecticut (6 percent), Florida (9.17 percent), Illinois (7 percent), Kansas (5.3 percent), Louisiana (3 percent), Massachusetts (5 percent), Michigan (6 percent), Minnesota (6.5 percent), Mississippi (7 percent), New Hampshire (7 percent), New Jersey (6 percent), Ohio (5 percent), Oklahoma (4.5 percent), Pennsylvania (6 percent), Rhode Island (7 percent), Texas (6.25 percent), Vermont (4.36 percent), Washington (6.5 percent), and Wisconsin (5 percent).

The state of New Mexico imposes a lower tax rate on interstate service than it does on intrastate service: 5 percent for intrastate and 4.25 percent for interstate. Tennessee also charges a lower intrastate rate (7 percent) than interstate rate (7.5 percent). In Maryland, a 5 percent tax is levied on mobile communications, 900-type phone services, and other select services. Interstate service is not taxed in North Carolina, and a higher tax rate, 6 percent, is applied to intrastate service than local exchange service, 3 percent. In South Carolina, intrastate service is taxed at 5 percent, while 900-type phone service is taxed at 10 percent. Hawaii taxes only interstate service at 4 percent. Telecommunication services may also be subject to local taxes.

Mailing Lists

Q 5:14 May states impose sales and use taxes on the use of mailing lists?

Generally, yes. However, if the mailing lists act as labels, they may qualify for exemption under a state's sales tax exemption for tangible personal property that becomes an ingredient or component part of other property sold at retail or otherwise exempt. For example, in *Crown Publishers v. Tully* [96 A.D.2d 990, 466 N.Y.S.2d 822 (3d Dep't 1983)], a New York court held that mailing labels were exempt from tax because they "were affixed to catalogues mailed to points outside New York."

The dispute between tax administrators and taxpayers over mailing lists reflects the continuing struggle in sales and use tax to distinguish between a sale of taxable tangible personal property and an intangible nontaxable service. The problem arises when taxpayers transfer intangibles through a tangible medium. Whether the transaction is taxable depends upon whether you focus on the thing being transferred (intangible information) or the mode of transfer (a tangible mailing list). New Jersey has ruled that the one-time rental of magnetic tapes containing mailing lists, which were transferred to the lessee's computer, was nontaxable because the real object of the transaction was information (the mailing lists), not the tapes themselves. [Spencer Gifts v. Director, 3 N.J. Tax 482 (1981)] Indiana recently ruled that the same transaction would be taxable in that state because the Department views the transaction as a sale of tangible personal property (the tapes) and not a sale of services. [Indiana Dept. of Rev., Ltr. of Findings: 01-0025]

Planning Point 5-7. Many states allow exemptions for shipping containers and packaging that is used to ship a product to its ultimate consumer. Frequently, the scope of these exemptions includes the labeling that is placed on the package or container. States also provide exemptions for printed advertising and promotional materials that are sent outside the state to promote a particular product. The labeling may become part of the advertising materials and thus qualify for the exemption. Finally, mailing lists that are purchased electronically or on a disk may be exempt from tax as a purchase of intangible property.

Internet or Electronic Commerce

Q 5:26 Are transmission-based services and content-based services taxed differently?

Traditionally, if a nontaxable service was coupled with a taxable sale of tangible personal property or other taxable service, the entire selling price was subject to sales tax. In fact, if the seller wishes to avoid charging tax on the entire transaction, many state statutes require separation of taxable and nontaxable goods or services on the sales invoice or bill. The convergence of voice, video, and data into one communications technology and the marketing of customized services into a single billing (called *bundling*) challenge the traditional approach to sales tax billing. The new technologies that enable electronic transmission providers to conjoin services with content providers illustrate the inadequacy of statutes passed in the 1930s and 1950s and raise new constitutional issues involving discrimination. For example, if traditional bookkeeping or tax services provided in an office setting are not taxable, then isn't it discriminatory to impose sales tax on the same services provided electronically by calling them a taxable computer service?

Some states are addressing the bundling issue by allowing telecommunications providers to exempt from tax charges, nontaxable services, even where those nontaxable services are not separately stated from the taxable charges. The telecom provider, however, must be able to satisfactorily separate such charges for internal and audit purposes. States recently adopting such an approach include Hawaii (Senate Bill (S.B.) 2885, SD-2, HD-1); Kansas (S.B. 1, July 2, 2001); Maryland (Md. Laws 2002, ch. 513 H.B. 378, effective July 1, 2002); and Michigan (Mich. Laws 2002, S.B. 477 and S.B. 1248, signed June 27, 2002).

In addition to the difficulties created by bundling, the new technologies in telecommunications make it difficult to distinguish between transmission- and content-based services even if separately billed and paid for. There is little controversy that basic telephone service, including cellular, is a taxable transmission-based service. However, disagreement exists whether fees for "enhanced services" such as caller-ID, call-waiting, voice-mail, conference calling, Internet access, and e-mail should also be taxed as no more than transmission services. Some argue that e-mail is more than basic transmission because it allows for changes in the transmitted data as well as temporary storage. Therefore, it more resembles content-based information and should not be taxed.

States that have adopted the definition of telecommunications found in the Telecommunications Act of 1996 generally have excluded e-mail and Internet access from sales tax while including such items as caller-ID, call-waiting, call-forwarding, and conference calling. The Act defines *telecommunications* as "the transmission between or among points specified by the user, of information of the user's choosing, without change in form or content of the information sent and received." Unfortunately, not all state and local governments have incorporated this definition into their statutes, and many have broader definitions that make it next to impossible to delineate between transmission-based and content-based services.

For example, the city of Denver defines *telecommunications services* as "the transmission of any two-way interactive electromagnetic communications including, but not limited to, voice, image, data and any other information, by the use of any means but not limited to wire, cable, fiber optical cable, microwave, radio wave or any combinations of such media. Telecommunications service includes, but is not limited to, basic local exchange telephone service, toll telephone service and teletypewriter business service, directory assistance, cellular mobile telephone or telecommunication service, specialized mobile radio and two-way pagers and paging service, including any form of mobile two-way communication." Under this definition Denver has argued that an answering service using a computer is taxable telecommunications, an answering service using humans is not. [D.R.M.C. § 53-24(26)] [For a detailed discussion of convergence, bundling, and its impact on sales and use tax, *see* Bruce Nelson & Dee Tagliavia, *Convergence and Bundling: The Impact on State and Local Telecommunications Taxes*, 5 St. & Loc. Tax Law. 21-41 (2000).]

Q 5:31 What is the possibility of federal intervention in the area of state taxation of electronic commerce?

Ever since the U.S. Supreme Court decision in *Quill* (*see* the discussion in Chapter 2, Q 2:5), Congress has had the authority to intervene and establish rules regarding the circumstances under which sales and use tax would have to be collected by out-of-state retailers. And since *Quill* was decided in 1992, legislation has been introduced every year in the U.S. Congress to establish nexus standards for sales and use tax, but to no avail. However, on October 21, 1998, the 105th Congress passed and President Clinton signed into law the Internet Tax Freedom Act (ITFA). The Act imposed a three-year moratorium, which was subsequently extended to November 1, 2003, on any taxes on Internet access and multiple and discriminatory taxes on electronic commerce. An exception to the moratorium for Internet access charges was provided for those states and local jurisdictions who were already taxing access charges. Initially, there were 12 states, the District of Columbia, and 12 Colorado home-rule cities that qualified for this "grandfathering" exception. Currently, there are only eight "grandfathered" states. They are Connecticut (tax phased out in 2002), New Mexico, North Dakota, Ohio, South Dakota, Tennessee, Texas and Wisconsin. (Texas imposes a 6.25%

state sales tax on Internet access but exempts the first $25 of monthly charges.) The 12 Colorado home-rule cities included Aspen, Aurora, Boulder, Commerce City, Durango, Fort Collins, Golden, Lafayette, Lakewood, Littleton, Thornton, and Wheatridge. (Despite being grandfathered, Tennessee's sales tax on Internet access was overturned in court on the grounds that the true object of the access fee was a nontaxable service, *i.e.*, the provision of information. [Prodigy Services Corp. v. Johnson, No. 98-1051-III (Davidson Ch. Ct. Mar. 19, 2002)] Iowa and the District of Columbia later enacted their own Internet legislation prohibiting sales tax on access charges. The moratorium expired in October 2001 but was extended on November 28, 2001, with President Bush's signing of H.R. 1552. The new bill extends the moratorium for two years and retains the original act's definition of Internet access and grandfather clause.

The ITFA also created a 19-member Advisory Commission on Electronic Commerce (ACEC). The Commission's mandate was to conduct a study of the Internet and Internet access and included as members eight representatives from state and local governments, eight representatives from industry, the United States Trade Representative, and the Secretaries of Commerce and Treasury. The Commission got off to a rocky start with disputes over the makeup of the membership. Dissension within the Commission continued, and the Commission was unable to include any formal recommendations with its final report because of insufficient votes within the body. The ACEC did, however, over the protests of several members, issue a majority report suggesting that the moratorium be extended for five years, that Internet access taxes be permanently banned, and that sales and use taxes be eliminated on all digitized goods and their non-digitized counterparts. After a flurry of activity and some initial press coverage, the ACEC and its report were quickly forgotten. The most recent efforts to simplify sales and use tax and establish a national standard for sales and use tax nexus is the Streamlined Sales Tax Project (SSTP) (*see* Chapter 21 for a discussion of the SSTP).

Chapter 6

Subjects of Sales and Use Taxes

Sales and use tax is imposed on the sale of tangible personal property and certain enumerated services. In this chapter we explore the subjects of sales and use tax—that is, the things and activities that constitute the scope of "tangible personal property" and "taxable services." These items vary from state to state and often reflect specific economic, geographic, social, or political forces unique to that state. It is no surprise then that the sales tax exemptions of agricultural and manufacturing states reflect their economic base, that Florida, which has no personal income tax, has a broader sales tax base than Colorado, or that Louisiana specifically exempts purchases of specialty items for Mardi Gras. In this chapter we explore the wonderful kaleidoscope of things states tax.

Tangible Personal Property

Q 6:2 How is the location of a sale of tangible personal property determined?

Because local sales and use tax rates vary considerably within a state, it is important to both the seller and the purchaser to properly determine just where the sale takes place and the appropriate local rate. There are a number of points in a sales tax transaction at which tax can be imposed. It can be imposed at the seller's place of business, the point of delivery, or the purchaser's domicile. Generally, the tax is imposed at the point at which title, possession, or control passes. After all, sales tax is a tax on a *sale*, the exchange of property, not the property itself. Therefore, the tax should theoretically attach wherever the sale is consummated. Accordingly, many state statutes provide that sales tax applies at the point at which title passes, whether that is the seller's location, the purchaser's location, or some other point. As a practical matter, however, most states follow the destination rule, which says that sales or use tax will generally apply at the point of destination. Such a position is consistent with the Uniform Commercial Code that dictates that in the absence of language to the contrary, title passes at destination. Nevertheless, the destination rule puts an enormous burden on the vendor to determine the correct local rate for each jurisdiction. As a consequence, some concessions have been made to mitigate the rule. California, for example, while following the general rule of assessing the tax where title passes, has afforded relief for vendors by specifically providing that for purposes of local sales taxes, all retail sales are deemed taxable at the seller's place of business. In addition, most states have adopted the "FTD" rule that allows sales tax to be charged at the point of order, not delivery, for businesses such as florists and pizza deliveries. Nevertheless, the "FTD" rule is under challenge by a florist who did not follow the standard. [*See* Proflowers, Inc. Petition for Redetermination (Cal. St. Bd. Equal. Aug. 1, 2002).]

Massachusetts taxpayers who attempted to avoid the state's sales tax by ordering an item from a Circuit City store in Massachusetts, but picking it up in New Hampshire (where there is no sales tax) were thwarted by the state's Appellate Tax Board. The Board rejected Circuit City's argument that only the order, not the purchase, took place in Massachusetts. The Board determined that the customer had an absolute right to possess the item upon payment in Massachusetts and, as a consequence, title passed in that state. [Circuit City Stores, Inc. v. Mass., No. F251413 (Mass. App. Feb. 11, 2002)]

Planning Point 6-2. Keep in mind that although the destination rule works well for goods that are shipped via common carrier to the customer, it does not apply to purchases in which the customer or the customer's carrier picks up the goods at the vendor's location. If the customer or the customer's agent takes possession or control of the goods sold, then, in most states, the sale is deemed to occur at the point at which title, possession, or control occurs. Therefore, the tax that would apply in this situation is the tax applicable in the location of the sale. If that rate happens to be lower than the rate imposed where the goods are ultimately used, a use tax could be due at that location, with a credit allowed for the sales tax actually paid.

Self-Constructed Assets

Q 6:4 How are self-constructed assets valued for use tax purposes?

If a manufacturer builds its own asset using materials drawn from inventory or otherwise purchased tax-free, the company may owe use tax on that asset. To decide whether the self-constructed asset is subject to use tax involves answering several questions. First, what is the nature of the machine? Is it used in manufacturing? Second, if the equipment is used in manufacturing, does that state in which the manufacturer does business provide a sales and use tax exemption for such machinery? Thirty-two states provide either a full or partial sales and use tax exemption for machinery and equipment used in manufacturing. If the machine qualifies for the state's exemption, there is no use tax liability on the self-constructed asset.

If the machine does not qualify for exemption or the state does not provide one, the question becomes one of determining the measure of the use tax due. There are three possibilities: (1) tax only the cost of materials; (2) tax the full cost, including any overhead and manufacturing labor; or (3) tax the fair market value. About one-third of the states report taxing only the cost of materials, five tax the materials cost plus an allocated portion of overhead, and four tax the fair market value. Other than using some combination of the three approaches, it is unclear what method the balance of the states follow. International Business Machines has won two victories against state revenue departments who attempted to assess use tax on more than the raw material cost of self-constructed assets. In Colorado the court said use tax is a complement to sales tax, and "the burden on the taxpayer should be no greater than necessary to compensate for the sales tax originally avoided on the purchases." [International Bus. Mach. v. Charnes, 601 P.2d 622, 624 (Colo. 1979); *see also* International Bus. Mach. v. Mich., 558 N.W.2d 456 (Mich. 1996) wherein the court agreed with the Colorado court's reasoning.]

There are several variables in calculating the use tax base for self-constructed assets. Some states assess use tax on the raw material cost of the components only. Other states use the retail value of the components rather than the cost. In either case, the labor cost to construct the asset may also be included in the taxable base. The following two tables identify the elements to be included in the tax base for both states that exempt machinery and equipment used in manufacturing or production and those states that do not.

Calculation of Tax Base in the States Not Providing an Exemption

I. Assets Used in Production

State	*Cost of Raw Materials*	*Cost of Raw Materials and Allocated Labor Costs*	*Retail Value of Component Parts*
Alabama [Ala. Code § 40-23-4]	Yes	No	No
District of Columbia [D.C. Code Ann. § 47-2002]	Yes	Yes	Yes

State	*Cost of Raw Materials*	*Cost of Raw Materials and Allocated Labor Costs*	*Retail Value of Component Parts*
Hawaii [Haw. Rev. Stat. § 238-1]	Yes	Yes	Yes
Louisiana [La. Rev. Stat. Ann. § 48:301(3)]	Yes	No	No
Minnesota [Minn. Stat. § 297A.68]	Yes	No	No
Mississippi [Miss. Code Ann. § 27-65-11]	Yes	No	No
Nebraska [Neb. Rev. Stat. §§ 77-2702.23, 77-2703]	Yes	No	No
Nevada [Nev. Rev. Stat. § 372]	Yes	No	No
New Mexico [N.M. Stat. Ann. § 7-9-7]	No	Yes	No
North Carolina [N.C. Gen. Stat. §§ 105-164.6]	Yes	No	No
South Dakota [S.D. Codified Laws Ann. §§ 10-45-2.2, 10-45-5.2, 10-46-5]	Yes	No	Yes
Utah [Utah Code Ann. § 59-12-104]	No	No	No
Washington [Wash. Rev. Code § 82-12.010(1)]	No	No	No
Wyoming [Wy. Stat. § 39-15-103]	Yes	No	Yes

Planning Point 6-3. Taxpayers may encounter problems when classifying assets as items used in the manufacturing process because of the different definitions of *use in manufacturing* that states use. Some states require "direct and/or exclusive" use in the manufacturing process in order for an item to qualify for the exemption, while others merely require predominant use in the manufacturing process. To limit their audit exposure, taxpayers engaged in multistate manufacturing activities should analyze each state's statute before assuming that a particular item of machinery and equipment will qualify for the exemption.

Calculation of Tax Base in All States

II. Assets Not Used in Production

State	*Cost of Raw Materials*	*Cost of Raw Materials and Allocated Labor Costs*	*Retail Value of Component Parts*
Alabama [Ala. Code § 40-23-4]	Yes	No	No
Arizona [Ariz. Rev. Stat. §§ 42-5159]	Yes	No	No
Arkansas [Ark. Code Ann. §§ 26-52-301, 26-52-402]	Yes	No	No
California [Cal. Rev. & Tax Code §§ 6051, 6201]	Yes	No	No
Colorado [Colo. Rev. Stat. § 39-26-114]	Yes	No	No
Connecticut [Conn. Gen. Stat. § 12-412(34)]	Yes	No	Yes
District of Columbia [D.C. Code Ann. § 47-2002]	Yes	Yes	Yes
Florida [Fla. Stat. § 212.08]	No	Yes	No
Georgia [Ga. Code Ann. § 48-8-3]	Yes	No	Yes
Hawaii [Haw. Rev. Stat. § 238-1]	Yes	Yes	Yes
Idaho [Idaho Code § 63-3621]	Yes	No	Yes
Illinois [35 Ill. Code Stat. 120 § 14]	No	No	No
Indiana [Ind. Code § 6-2.5-4-2]	Yes	No	Yes
Iowa [Iowa Code §§ 422.45, 423.4]	Yes	No	No
Kansas [Kan. Stat. Ann. § 79-3606(kk)]	Yes	No	Yes
Kentucky [Ky. Rev. Stat. Ann. § 139.470]	Yes	No	No
Louisiana [La. Rev. Stat. Ann. § 48:301(3)]	Yes	No	No
Maine [Me. Rev. Stat. Ann. tit. 36 § 1760.31]	Yes	No	No
Maryland [Md. Tax Gen. Code Ann. § 11-101(i)(2)]	Yes	No	No
Massachusetts [Mass. Gen. Laws ch. 64H, §§ 6(r), 6(s)]	Yes	No	No
Michigan [Mich. Comp. Laws § 205.94]	Yes	Yes	No
Minnesota [Minn. Stat. § 297A.12]	Yes	No	No

State	*Cost of Raw Materials*	*Cost of Raw Materials and Allocated Labor Costs*	*Retail Value of Component Parts*
Mississippi [Miss. Code Ann. § 27-65-11]	Yes	No	No
Missouri [Mo. Rev. Stat. § 144.030]	No	No	No
Nebraska [Neb. Rev. Stat. §§ 77-2702.23, 77-2703]	Yes	No	No
Nevada [Nev. Rev. Stat. § 372]	Yes	No	No
New Jersey [N.J. Stat. Ann. § 54-32B-6]	Yes	Yes	No
New Mexico [N.M. Stat. Ann. § 7-9-7]	No	Yes	No
New York [N.Y. Tax Law §§ 1105(a), 1115(a)(12)]	Yes	No	No
North Carolina [N.C. Gen. Stat. §§ 105, 164.6]	Yes	No	No
North Dakota [N.D. Cent. Code § 57-40.2-02.1]	Yes	No	No
Ohio [Ohio Rev. Code Ann. § 5741.01(G)]	No	Yes	No
Oklahoma [Okla. Stat. tit. 68, § 1359]	Yes	No	No
Pennsylvania [61 Pa. Cons. Stat. § 32.1]	Yes	No	No
Rhode Island [R.I. Gen. Laws §§ 44-18-11, 44-18-30]	Yes	No	No
South Carolina [S.C. Code Ann. § 12-36-110]	Yes	No	No
South Dakota [S.D. Codified Laws Ann. §§ 10-45-2.2, 10-46-5, 10-45-5.2]	Yes	Yes	No
Tennessee [Tenn. Code Ann. § 67-6-102(13)]	Yes	No	No
Texas [Tex. Code Ann. §§ 151.005, 151.007, 151.318]	Yes	No	No
Utah [Utah Code Ann. § 59-12-104]	Yes	No	No
Vermont [Vt. Stat. Ann. § 9741(14)]	Yes	No	Yes (if corp. sells similar parts)
Virginia [Va. Code Ann. § 58.1-609.3]	Yes	No	No
Washington [Wash. Rev. Code § 82-12.010(1)]	Yes	Yes	Yes
West Virginia [W. Va. Code § 11-15-9(b)]	No	Yes	No

State	*Cost of Raw Materials*	*Cost of Raw Materials and Allocated Labor Costs*	*Retail Value of Component Parts*
Wisconsin [Wis. Stat. § 77.53(1)]	Yes	No	No
Wyoming [Wyo. Stat. § 39-15-103]	Yes	No	Yes

Computer Software

Q 6:13 Are sales of custom software developed for a specific client subject to sales tax?

Generally not. Most states do not tax custom software because it is deemed to be either a purchase of a nontaxable service or an intangible. At its most basic level, custom software is specifically written for the exclusive use of one particular user. The following states and the District of Columbia, however, do tax custom software: Arkansas, Connecticut, Hawaii, Kansas, Louisiana, Mississippi, Nebraska, New Mexico, South Carolina, South Dakota, Tennessee, Texas, and West Virginia. Software used in manufacturing may qualify for exemption in those states that exempt machinery and equipment used in manufacturing.

Q 6:15 What arguments can a taxpayer use in claiming that software is nontaxable?

Most of the successful arguments claiming that software is nontaxable are variations of the "true object" test. The true object test is often used when the transaction involves a significant service element mixed with tangible personal property—for example, the purchase of a mailing list. The taxpayer looks at the information transferred and argues that no sales tax is due because it is the sale of an intangible. The tax administrator focuses instead on the way the information was transferred and sees the sale of tangible personal property. [Globe Life & Accident Ins. v. Tax Comm'r, No. 83,426 (Okla. Mar. 19, 1996)] It is the same issue with computer software. The taxpayer focuses on the intangible intellectual property, while the tax administrator looks to the method of delivery. The true object test asks, "What is it the customer really wants? Is it the services per se? Or is it the tangible personal property created by those services?'' The answers are not always clear.

Arguments advanced under the true object test include using alternative means of delivery, the incidental cost of the tangible personal property, the fact that the intellectual property can be divorced from the tangible personal property, and the licensing of intangibles. Many of these arguments were first developed in the property and income tax arenas, particularly with respect to the federal Investment Tax Credit, which was deleted from the Internal Revenue Code in 1986. As a consequence the successful use of the arguments in sales tax has been mixed.

Some businesses have successfully supported their use of the true object test by pointing to the fact that they are indifferent as to how the software is delivered. It can be delivered on tape, disk, or electronically over the Internet. They argue that "it doesn't matter how it is delivered. The true object of this transaction isn't the tangible personal property but rather a nontaxable intangible, the computer code.'' Taxpayers won some early decisions using this argument. [Commerce Union Bank v. Tidwell, 538 S.W.2d 405 (Tenn. 1976); Bullock v. Statistical Tabulating, 549 S.W.2d 166 (Tex. 1977)] Currently, some states exempt even canned software if it is delivered electronically. The states include Arkansas, California, Florida, Georgia, Iowa, Kentucky, Maryland, Missouri, Nevada, New Jersey, Oklahoma, Pennsylvania, Rhode Island, Vermont, Virginia, and West Virginia.

A second argument in the true object test arsenal is to point out that the value of the tangible personal property is incidental and insignificant in relationship to the value of the intangible being conveyed by the tangible personal property. After all, a $30,000 software program can be conveyed on a CD worth at most a dollar or two. The extreme difference in value is further evidence that it is not the taxable tangible personal property but instead intangible intellectual property or services, that is the true object of the transaction. In Missouri a taxpayer paid tax on blank tapes worth $50 but not the $135,000 cost for the computer programs. The Missouri Supreme Court ruled for the taxpayer, determining that the tapes were incidental to the purchase. The real object of the taxpayer's purchase was the nontaxable intangible information on the tapes. [James v. Tres Computer Serv., 642 S.W.2d 347 (Mo. 1982)] That this argument is still useful was recently supported in Connecticut where purchases of informational databases were determined to be the purchase of information rather than the magnetic tapes used to deliver the information. [NERAC Inc. v. Comm'r, No. CV99 0493548S (Conn. Super. Ct. Nov. 30, 2001)]

Another successful argument proposes that where the tangible personal property can be severed and discarded or returned, that is evidence that the real object of the transaction was not the tangible personal property but the intangible information. In one of the oldest cases using this argument, Universal Computer argued that no property tax was due on punch cards used to enter information into a computer and then thrown away. [District of Columbia v. Universal Computer, 465 F.2d 615 (D.C. 1972)]

Finally, some taxpayers have argued that a purchase of computer software is never really a sale because title never passes. What is really being sold is a nontaxable intangible license to use a computer program. For anyone who has ever read the agreement contained in even canned software, this argument seems to have merit. Unfortunately the argument rests on the assumption that the right to use tangible personal property can be separated from the property itself, a position rejected by more than one court. [Columbia Pictures v. Tax Comm'n, 410 A.2d 457 (Conn. 1979); American Multi-Cinema v. Westminster, 910 P.2d 64 (Colo. Ct. App. 1995), *cert. denied* (1996)]

While many taxpayers have been successful with arguing the elements of the true object test, many others have not. Tax administrators have responded to the alternative delivery argument by pointing out that the taxability of a transaction should not be determined by its mode of delivery. If the purchaser has the right to maintain a copy in any format on her own computer, Colorado, for example, holds that canned software is taxable, even if received over the Internet. [Colo. Rev. Policy Position 1-97] When confronted with the argument that the tangible personal property in a software purchase is inconsequential, tax administrators ask how that is any different from the purchase of a $2,000 custom suit or a million-dollar painting. As a consequence, many states have changed their laws or adopted new statutes and regulations specifically addressing some of these issues. Nevertheless, the growth in e-commerce and the conversion of books, CDs, movies, and other information into digital format coupled with diminishing state revenues will ensure that these issues will be debated and litigated for some time to come.

[For a general overview of these and related issues, see James Smith, *State Taxation of Electronic Commerce: Part 1*, 17 J. of St. Tax'n 1 (1998); James Smith, *State Taxation of Electronic Commerce: Part 2*, 17 J. of St. Tax'n 1 (1999); Bruce Harvey, *Canned and Custom Software: The Taxability Issue*, 15 J. of St. Tax'n 81 (1997); J. Elaine Bialczak, *The True Object Test Applied to States' Sales Tax on Information Services*, 10 J. of St. Tax'n 46 (1991); Dane and Bruskin, *The Sales Tax Status of Software Revisited*, 4 J. of St. Tax'n 53 (1985); Fench and Koeppel, *Computer Software and Sales Taxation*, 3 J. of St. Tax'n 165 (1984); Hanlon, *Computer Software and Sales Taxes: New Cases Take an Old Direction*, 25 J. of St. Tax'n 315 (1984).]

Planning Point 6-10. States that exempt prewritten programs transmitted by intangible means have established a precedent that may pose limitations on their ability to tax transactions that occur over the Internet. For example, if a purchaser downloads software from a Web site on the Internet, it would be exempt from sales tax in those states. It could be argued that downloading music, books, magazines, or art are fundamentally no different. Although all these purchases would be taxable if purchased in a conventional manner, purchasing the electronic version of these items would not. This result may create new challenges for the sales taxation structure of many states.

Planning Point 6-11. To determine whether the buyer has purchased canned or custom software, the states use a number of factors to make the distinction, including the following:

- Degree of pre-sale consultation and analysis of a user's requirements
- Whether programs are loaded onto the purchaser's computer by the purchaser or vendor
- Degree of training and written documentation required for successful operation
- Amount of enhancement and maintenance support required for continued usefulness of the program
- Cost of the program
- Whether the program includes basic operational programs or prewritten programs
- If the program involves an existing program that is modified, the degree of modification to the program by the vendor.

Q 6:18 Are computer software maintenance contracts subject to sales tax?

It depends. Whether or not software maintenance contracts are subject to sales tax depends on a state's general rules for all maintenance contracts, whether the software is canned or custom, and the components of the contract itself, including upgrades and support services such as a "help desk."

Some states distinguish between two types of maintenance and warranty contracts. The first, which comes bundled as part of the purchase price of the property, is often called a "mandatory" maintenance or warranty contract. Because the customer has paid tax on the purchase price (including the warranty), there is no additional tax due on repair parts provided later to fulfill the contract. The second type of maintenance or warranty contract is called an "optional" maintenance or warranty contract. The maintenance is optional because it is separately stated and the customer may choose to buy it or not. Examples include extended warranties offered on everything from televisions and washing machines to cars. As a service agreement, most states do not tax these contracts. However, any parts used to fulfill the contract are taxable. The different treatment afforded these two types of contracts, coupled with the canned/custom distinction and the scope of a state's taxable services, accounts for most of the variable treatment of maintenance contracts.

Most states impose sales and use tax on computer software maintenance contracts. Software maintenance contracts are exempt in Arizona, Arkansas, Colorado, Georgia, Hawaii (if the service is rendered in the state), Illinois, Indiana, Kentucky, Louisiana, Maine, Massachusetts, Michigan, Missouri, Nevada, New York, North Carolina, Oklahoma, Rhode Island, Vermont, Washington, and Wyoming. Some states impose tax only if the contract is mandatory. If the software maintenance contract includes software updates, most states will assess sales and use tax.

"Help-desk" services are generally billed annually and, as services, are not taxed in most states. The service usually includes toll-free numbers a customer can call to speak live with software and computer consultants who try to solve the customer's hardware or software problems. Help-desk fees are taxable in Hawaii, Nebraska (if part of a maintenance contract), New Mexico, South Dakota, Tennessee, Texas, and the District of Columbia. If the help-desk service provider is not in the same state as the customer, there may be a question of where the taxable service occurs and which state will have jurisdiction to tax the transaction.

Containers and Packing Materials

Q 6:26 What are the procedures for state sales and use taxation of packing materials?

Purchases of containers and packing materials are usually exempt under either a state's sale-for-resale exemption or by specific statute or regulation. Forty-three states and the District of Columbia exempt some combination of nonreturnable containers and packing materials, including shrink-wrap, bags, cans, twine, gummed tape, boxes, bottles, drums, and cartons, that are sold with the products to the final consumer. Hawaii and Massachusetts are the exceptions. Careful attention must be paid to the scope and precise nature of each state's definition of qualifying containers and packing materials. For example, Texas exempts containers but not wrapping, packing, and packaging. Other states limit their exemption to only containers and packaging used to deliver the product to the end user. Sometimes taxability is dependent upon whether the materials are returned. If not returned, the items may qualify for exemption, not as packing material, but as ingredient or component parts of the property being sold. Kansas recently ruled that pallets, labels, wrapping, tape, and perhaps even ice if not returned, would be exempt from tax as ingredients. [Kan. Dept. of Rev., Ltr. Rul. P-2002-001 (Jan. 7, 2002)] Pallets and shipping materials used to deliver the product from wholesaler or manufacturer to retailer often do not qualify. Court decisions in different states but ruling on identical or similar language have reached inconsistent positions. [For a good summary of two theoretically distinct approaches to the issue of taxing containers and packaging, see American Molasses v. McGoldrick & Sterling Bag, 22 N.E.2d 369 (N.Y. 1939), and District of Columbia v. Seven-Up, 214 F.2d 197 (D.C. Cir. 1954), *cert. denied,* 347 U.S. 989 (1954).]

Planning Point 6-14. In many states, the distinction between taxable and nontaxable shipping and packing materials is driven by whether the item is returnable or nonreturnable, even if used to ship the product to the customer. For example, if the packing and shipping materials are returnable, such as barrels, pallets, kegs, or crates, then the item is taxable, regardless of whether it is used to ship the product to the customer. In other states, the returnable/nonreturnable distinction does not affect the tax treatment of the item, so long as the item is used to ship the product to the customer.

Planning Point 6-15. Keep in mind that if the underlying shipping container or aid is taxable, any repairs to returnable shipping containers and aids are also subject to tax. Many taxpayers fail to institute procedures to review such repairs for use tax and, as a result, have unnecessary use tax exposure upon audit.

Leased Property

Q 6:29 Are leases of tangible personal property subject to sales tax?

Yes. Forty-three of the forty-five states with a sales and use tax, and the District of Columbia, tax leases of tangible personal property. Illinois and Ohio are the exceptions. In Illinois the lease itself is not taxed because the lessor must pay a lessor's use tax on the initial purchase price of the property. Effective February 1, 2002, Ohio sales tax must be paid up front at inception on certain vehicle leases and leases used mainly in business. [Ohio H.B. 405 (Dec. 13, 2001)] Several states exempt motor vehicle leases from their general sales and use tax and instead assess specific vehicle rental or tourism taxes in their place. Those states include Illinois, Kentucky, Louisiana, New Mexico, North Carolina, North Dakota, Oklahoma, Texas, Vermont, and Virginia.

The difficulties in properly applying sales and use tax to leases lie in determining (1) whether the transaction is really a lease or a sale; (2) the location of the property; (3) the location of the lessee; (4) the taxable base; and (5) specific industry standards.

Lease or sale. The first determination that must be made is whether or not the transaction is a true lease or a conditional sale. In a true lease, the lessor is, and remains, the owner of the property, and the lessee is paying rent. At the end of the lease, the equipment is either returned to the lessor or purchased from the lessor at its fair market value. A *conditional sale* is a financing arrangement in which the lessee acquires title to the property, either at the inception of the lease or its end, for a nominal price that is unrelated to the property's fair market value.

Part of the problem with the proper sales and use tax treatment of leases is its terminology. Leasing is multidisciplinary because it crosses several areas, including finance, accounting, law, and tax. Each discipline has its own approach to leasing, its own terminology, and its own acronyms. For example, it is possible to structure a lease (called a synthetic lease) as an operating lease for financial statement purposes and as a loan for income tax purposes.

The large body of law, both statutory and case law, related to leases is beyond the scope of this text. Nevertheless, the beginning point for any analysis is the guidance offered by the IRS in Revenue Ruling 55-540 [55-2 C.B. 39] and Revenue Procedures 75-21 [75-1 C.B. 715], 75-28 [75-1 C.B. 752], 76-30 [76-2 C.B. 647], and 79-48 [79-1 C.B. 569]. In many cases, the determination is based on the leases' specific facts and circumstances. Many states follow federal guidelines in drawing their own distinctions between leases and sales. However, other states provide their own definition of a lease. For example, one of California's requirements for true lease treatment is that the nominal purchase option at the end of the lease be greater than $100 or 1 percent of the total contract price. [Cal. Rev. & Tax Code § 6006.3] Many of the smaller states have yet to address the variety of leasing arrangements available. For example, Florida has issued a ruling providing that synthetic leases are exempt from sales and use tax. [Fla. Tech. Assistance Advisement 00A-041 (July 25, 2000)] Illinois taxes synthetic leases as conditional sales, not true leases. [Ill. Dept. of Rev., Ltr. Rul. ST 02-0006-PLR (Mar. 21, 2002)] Many smaller states such as Colorado and Wyoming have yet to address the issue.

Location of the property and lessee. The location of the property and lessee raises questions of nexus (*see* Qs 2:6 and 2:10) for lessor and lessee as well as the proper rate of tax to be applied to the rent. Some of the questions include the following: Does the property create nexus for either or both the lessor and lessee? What are the consequences if the property is leased in one state and immediately taken and put to use in another state? Which state's tax applies? The answers to these questions vary from state to state and by property type. For example, licensed motor vehicles, and mobile equipment, usually receive treatment different from that given other tangible personal property. Plated or licensed vehicles are generally taxed where registered. Special mobile equipment such as cranes, however, often prove to be exceptions to the rule. Nineteen states report that occasional use of rented mobile property by lessees in their states is not taxable. Those states include Colorado, Connecticut, Idaho, Indiana, Kentucky, Louisiana, Maine, Michigan, Mississippi, New Mexico, North Dakota, Ohio, Oklahoma, South Carolina, Texas, Vermont, Virginia, Wisconsin, and Wyoming. Occasional use of rented mobile property is taxable in Alabama, Arizona, Arkansas, Florida, Georgia, Hawaii, Iowa, Kansas, Maryland, Massachusetts, Minnesota, Missouri, Nebraska, Nevada, New Jersey, Pennsylvania, Rhode Island, South Dakota, Tennessee, Utah, Washington, and the District of Columbia.

Taxable base. Defining the taxable base for lease payments varies from state to state. Some of the items that may or may not be taxable include late charges and related interest, prepayment penalties, insurance payments, delivery and pickup fees, collection costs, and property taxes. These items may be taxable regardless of whether they are separately stated or paid by the lessor or, in the case of property taxes, paid directly by the lessee. Prepayment penalties are taxable in Alabama, Arizona, Arkansas, California, Connecticut, Georgia, Hawaii, Iowa, Louisiana, Minnesota, Mississippi, New Jersey, Ohio, Oklahoma, Pennsylvania, South Carolina, South Dakota, Tennessee, Texas, Washington, and Wisconsin. Separately stated optional insurance is taxable in Alabama, Arkansas, Hawaii, Indiana, Kansas, Mississippi, Ohio, Oklahoma, Pennsylvania, Rhode Island, South Carolina, South Dakota, Tennessee, Utah, Virginia, Washington, and West Virginia.

Industry standards. Collection and reporting obligations can also change depending upon the classification of the lessor. The lessor may be strictly a vehicle lessor, a financial institution, a third-party lessor, an OEM (original equipment manufacturer) lessor, or simply a construction company with some idle equipment.

In fact, given the differences between the states, the segments of the leasing industry, the types of leases, and the taxable base, perhaps the better answer to whether or not leases are subject to sales and use tax is, "It depends."

Planning Point 6-17. Generally, leases meeting the definition of a *lease* under Generally Accepted Accounting Principles (GAAP) or the Internal Revenue Code (Code) will qualify as true leases for sales and use tax purposes. This generally requires that the lessee purchase the equipment for a residual value at the end of the lease that approximates the equipment's fair market value.

Planning Point 6-18. In some states, additional charges can be recharacterized as a lease payment that is subject to tax. For example, with equipment leases it is fairly common to include, as an additional charge, the amount of property taxes paid by the lessor on the equipment. If that is done, the charge is recharacterized as a lease payment and is subject to tax. Taxpayers engaged in leasing need to be aware of the treatment of these additional charges to avoid under-billing the sales tax on their lease receipts.

Planning Point 6-19. In transactions where the lease constitutes a sale, the vendor should remit tax on the "selling price" of the equipment included in the lease. In such cases, the interest component, inherent in the transaction, would not be subject to tax. However, for true leases, as noted above, the interest component would be subject to tax.

Machinery and Equipment

Q 6:32 What constitutes manufacturing?

Manufacturing comprises so many different activities that it is no surprise that the definition, interpretation, and application of the term varies from state to state. For example, all manufacturing probably includes some processing and/or fabrication, but not all fabrication or processing is manufacturing. Similar questions arise over refining, assembly, and construction. Tracing the outlines of manufacturing's definition and scope has become almost a cottage industry for tax administrators and professionals alike.

The lodestone for most states' definitions of the term *manufacturing* is the U.S. Supreme Court's statement that "manufacturing implies a change . . . there must be a transformation; a new and different article must emerge, having a distinctive name, character, or use.'' [East Tex. Motor Freight Lines v. Frozen Foods Express, 351 U.S. 49 (1956)] Unfortunately, there has been little agreement in interpreting the Court's definition. For example, in *Stone v. Tax Commissioner* [227 A.2d 76 (Conn. 1967)], meat processing did not qualify as manufacturing. However, in Missouri meat processing does qualify as manufacturing. [Wilson & Co. v. Department of Rev., 531 S.W.2d 752 (Mo. 1976)] In Wisconsin, mixing sand, gravel, and water together to make cement qualified as manufacturing, but mixing syrup and water together to make sodas, or ice cream and chocolate powder to make shakes in Oklahoma is not manufacturing. [*See* Valley Ready Mixed Concrete v. Wisconsin, No. 84-CV-6724 (Wis. Cir. Ct. May 2, 1985); McDonald's v. Oklahoma, 563 P.2d 635 (Okla. 1977)] Making snow in New York is not manufacturing, but it is in Pennsylvania. [Shanty Hollow v. New York, 111 A.D.2d 68, *leave to appeal denied,* 489 N.E.2d 256 (N.Y. 1985); Ski Roundtop v. Commonwealth, 553 A.2d 934 (Pa. 1989).] Rebuilding machine tools has been ruled to constitute manufacturing, but rebuilding engines has not. [*See* Eastern Machinery v. Peck, 114 N.E.2d 55 (Ohio 1953) and Beasley Industries v. Commonwealth, No. 1198, CD 1976 (Pa. 1988).] Pennsylvania, for example, has challenged the processing of honey, the pasteurization of milk, and the milling of flour. [*See* Stewart Honeybee Products v. Commonwealth, 562 A.2d 1015 (Pa. 1989); Rieck-McJunkin Dairy v. Pittsburgh Sch. Dist., 66 A.2d 295 (Pa. 1949); American Ice v. Commonwealth, 178 A.2d 768 (Pa. 1962).] In Massachusetts, processing raw vegetables through cleaning, coring, peeling, and shredding, to produce prepackaged vegetable packets for sale to supermarkets and grocery stores, qualifies one as a manufacturer. [Noreast Fresh, Inc. v. Comm'r of Rev., 737 N.E.2d 17 (Mass. Ct. App. 2000)]

Once a taxpayer's activity meets the definition of manufacturing, there remain additional questions, including identifying the beginning and ending of the manufacturing process, and determining whether equipment involved in activities such as testing, research and development, quality control, pollution control, safety, temperature control, repair and maintenance, storage, and transport (forklifts, loaders, and conveyor belts) qualifies as machinery and equipment used in manufacturing. Needless to say, the answers vary from state to state. Some recent examples of the variety and range of decisions include:

- Kiln sticks placed between wood layers to dry logs for sale as lumber qualified for Alabama's reduced tax rate for manufacturing machinery because the stacking sticks performed "an integral function" and was "part and parcel of the machinery used in production." [Overseas Hardwoods Co. Inv. v. Ala., Admin. Law Div., No. S. 00-664 (Oct. 1, 2001)]
- Lubricants used to protect machine parts from heat damage and friction qualified for Alabama's reduced tax rate for manufacturing machinery because protecting machine parts during manufacturing constituted a direct, essential, and necessary function in the manufacturing process. [NTN Bower Corp. v. Alabama, Admin. Law Div., No. S. 01-237 (Oct. 1, 2001)]
- Machinery used to mass duplicate canned software qualified for Connecticut's manufacturing machinery exemption because the encoding of blank disks transformed the disk into a new product. Machinery used for software design and development, however, does not qualify for the state's exemption. [Connecticut Policy Statement 2001-12 (Oct. 13, 2001)] In Kansas, however, computer hardware, but not software, used in engineering, research and development, and product design qualified for the state's sales tax exemption as "peripheral equipment." [Kan. Dep't of Rev., P-2002-045 (June 5, 2002)]
- Electricity used to convert ammonia gas to a liquid to chill air in frozen food warehouses qualified for the state's manufacturing exemption because the transformation of the ammonia was used to produce a product—chilled air. [Interstate Warehousing Inc. v. Ind., 764 N.E.2d 313 (Ind. Tax Court 2002). *See also* Mid-America Energy Resources Inc. v. Dep't of State Rev., 681 N.E. 2d 259 (Ind. Tax Court 1997) for a similar decision.]
- Sterilization equipment that did not act upon the product, but sterilized the bottles and containers used to hold the product, qualified for Kansas's manufacturing machinery exemption because the equipment was used in packaging, an integral part of production. [Kan. Dep't Rev. Op. Ltr. O-2001-024 (Oct. 29, 2001)]
- Piping, meters, equipment, and holding tanks used to treat, bury, or store waste water from a production process qualified for New York's manufacturing machinery sales tax exemption. [N.Y. Dep't of Tax'n, TSB-A-02(27)S (July 12, 2002)]

Planning Point 6-20. In most states, manufacturing begins when the item is removed from its first point of storage and ends when the item is removed at the end of the manufacturing process and placed in finished goods storage. If some activity occurs at the first point of storage, such has heating, cooling, or mixing raw materials, the manufacturing process may be considered under way at that point. Most states consider the shipping and receiving areas to be outside the manufacturing process. However, if some of the receiving inspection activities can be undertaken after the goods have entered into the manufacturing process, the activities may be considered exempt.

Q 6:33 For an exemption from sales and use tax, must production equipment be directly used in the manufacturing operation?

Yes. Most states require that for machinery and equipment to qualify for the sales and use tax manufacturing exemption, it must be used directly, exclusively, primarily, predominantly, or some combination of the preceding in manufacturing tangible personal property for sale or profit. How *direct, exclusive, primarily,* and *predominantly* are defined varies from state to state. Typically, *direct use* requires that the machine actually come into contact with, act upon, or be involved with the raw material being manufactured. In other states, the equipment must be essential, but it need not act directly upon the product. Seventeen states require that the machinery or equipment be used directly (Arizona, Arkansas, Connecticut, Georgia, Illinois, Indiana, Kentucky, Maine, Michigan, Minnesota (for refund purposes), Missouri (for new or expanded plants only), North Carolina, North Dakota, Oklahoma, Rhode Island, Virginia, and Washington). The Missouri Supreme Court recently ruled that computer equipment used in the production of printed materials qualified for the state's sales tax exemption for machinery used in manufacturing. Even though the computers were several miles from the actual printing plant, the machines were still used directly in manufacturing. [DST Systems Inc. v. Dir. of Rev., 43 S.W.3d 799 (Mo. 2001)] Seven states require direct and exclusive use (Alabama, Florida, Massachusetts, Pennsylvania, Vermont, West Virginia, and Wisconsin (but permits a 5 percent nonmanufacturing use)). In Pennsylvania, for example, machinery used to repackage products at a distribution center did not qualify for the machinery exemption because none of the products were manufactured at the center. [AMP Inc. v. Pa., No. 837 F.R. 1998 (Pa. Commw. Ct. Feb. 22, 2002)] *Exclusive use* is generally defined as sole, unshared, undivided, 100 percent utilization in the manufacturing process. A few states will accept *de minimis* nonmanufacturing use of the machinery or equipment, others will not. Three states report that the machinery must be used directly and primarily in manufacturing (Idaho, Iowa, and New Jersey). Colorado, Maryland, New York, and Texas require direct and predominant use, while Ohio requires only primary and South Carolina direct and substantial use in manufacturing. (New York recently ruled that equipment used to load and unload raw material qualified for the state's sales tax exemption where the production process had already begun. [N.Y. Dep't of Tax'n, TSB-A-02(17)S (June 26, 2002)] Tennessee requires that the machinery be both primarily used in manufacturing and necessary. Kansas requires that the machinery be an integral or essential part of manufacturing (but *see* Q 6:32 for recent Kansas decisions). *Primary or predominant use* is generally defined as meaning more than 50 percent of the machine or equipment's use must be in manufacturing or production.

Planning Point 6-21. Although many states offer exemptions for production equipment, few extend the exemption to repair or replacement parts. In states that include repair or replacement parts in the exemption, the same usage tests generally apply to the repair or replacement parts. If an exact determination of usage cannot be made, parts can be apportioned between taxable and nontaxable uses. For example, if materials handling equipment qualifies as exempt and there are ten forklifts used in the process and five used outside the manufacturing process, two-thirds of the repair parts would be exempt and one-third would be taxable. Of course, if an exact determination of usage can be made, that is preferable.

Mergers, Consolidations, Acquisitions, Liquidations, or Incorporations

Q 6:39 Are sales taxes imposed on mergers, consolidations, acquisitions, liquidations, or incorporations?

Generally, no. Mergers, consolidations, acquisitions, liquidations, reorganizations, or incorporations are usually exempt because (1) they are excluded from the definition of a sale; (2) they are sales of intangibles, not tangible property; and (3) they are specifically exempted by statute. Exclusions of mergers and the like can be either quite broad or very specific. California's exclusion is quite general, excluding "any transfer of all or substantially all the property held or used by a person in the course of such activities when after such transfer the real or ultimate ownership is substantially similar to that which existed before such transfer." [Cal. Rev. & Tax Code § 6006.5 (b)] Colorado's exclusion is very specific detailing each type of transaction excluded with separate paragraphs for IRC § 351 transfers, partnership interest exchanges, and IRC § 368 reorganizations. To qualify for exclusion the transaction must meet the statutory requirements precisely. [Colo. Rev. Stat. § 39-26-102(10)] Any consideration received in an otherwise tax-free transfer or reorganization may taint the entire transaction thereby subjecting it to sales tax. For example, a parent corporation's transfer of a division's assets and liabilities solely in exchange for stock was a taxable retail sale because the liabilities transferred constituted consideration. [Beatrice v. State Bd. of Equal., 863 P.2d 683 (Cal. 1993)] "Midstream" IRC Section 351 transfers or asset transfers to already existing corporations may not qualify as exempt sales for sales tax. An asset for stock transfer by a sole proprietor to a corporation solely owned by that individual did not qualify for exempt treatment in New York. [*In re* R.E. Weichbrodt, Inc., No. 817950 (N.Y. Div. Tax App., ALJ Div., Jan. 31, 2002)]

A liquidation might also be exempt under a state's isolated, casual, or occasional sale exemption. These exemptions are generally restricted to nonrecurring sales outside the vendor's ordinary trade or business. Some states limit the number of casual or isolated sales a vendor may have each year, while other states limit the exemption to entities going out of business.

Two exceptions to the general sales and use tax exemptions for mergers, consolidations, acquisitions, reorganizations, and casual or isolated sales are purchases of inventory and transfers of motor vehicles. Bulk sale or occasional sale exemptions usually do not cover inventory. Thus, assuming the purchase of inventory is for resale, a sale-for-resale exemption must be used to avoid taxation. The transfer of motor vehicles, even in an otherwise tax-free merger or consolidation, is often taxable because of the change in titling and licensing, although some states provide exemptions for related-party transfers.

Thirty states and the District of Columbia exempt from sales and use tax asset acquisition purchases as casual, bulk, or isolated sales (Alabama, Arizona, Arkansas, Connecticut, Florida, Georgia, Hawaii, Idaho, Illinois (unless the taxpayer sells like-kind property and the purchase was for use or consumption), Indiana, Maine, Michigan, Minnesota, Mississippi, Missouri, Nevada, New Jersey, New Mexico, North Carolina, North Dakota, Pennsylvania, Rhode Island, South Dakota, Tennessee, Texas, Utah, Vermont, Virginia, West Virginia, and Wyoming).

The following states do not exempt acquisitions through asset purchase: California, Colorado, Iowa, Kentucky, Maryland, Massachusetts, Michigan, Nebraska, New York, Ohio (but may qualify as casual sales), Oklahoma, Texas (but may qualify as occasional sale), Washington, and Wisconsin (with some exceptions). Generally, liquidations of corporations are exempt from sales and use tax. Liquidations are taxable in Iowa, Kentucky, Michigan, Nevada, Oklahoma, South Carolina, Utah, Washington, and Wyoming. Incorporations are exempt from sales and use taxation everywhere except Iowa, and perhaps the home-rule city of Denver, Colorado.

Most states tax transfers of tangible personal property to an existing subsidiary. The District of Columbia and the following states exempt transfers of tangible personal property to an existing subsidiary: Alabama, Arizona, California, Connecticut, Idaho, Illinois, Minnesota, Missouri, Nebraska, New Mexico, New York, North Carolina, North Dakota, Pennsylvania, South Dakota, Tennessee, Vermont, Washington, West Virginia, and Wyoming.

Care must also be taken upon entering three-party federal IRC Section 1031 exchanges. There is little guidance among the states as to whether the third-party intermediary facilitating the exchange must hold a sales tax license or execute resale certificates. Recent rulings in New York, South Carolina, and Iowa have held that the intermediary in a qualifying Section 1031 exchange will be ignored for sales and use tax purposes. [*See* N.Y. Dep't of Tax'n, TSB-A-02(20)S (June 26, 2002); S.C. Dep't of Rev., Priv. Rev. Op. No. 02-2 (March 11, 2002); and Matter of Ford Motor Credit Co., No. 01-30-G-0227 (Iowa Dep't of Rev. Nov. 20, 2001).]

Planning Point 6-25. Taxpayers selling assets in bulk frequently fail to recognize that the sale (even if made as a division or segment of another business) constitutes a taxable event for sales and use tax purposes. The sales tax would only apply to the "hard" assets that were sold in the transaction. Therefore, any intangibles, such as patents, know-how, or goodwill, would not be subject to tax. However other assets, such as office equipment, manufacturing machinery and equipment (unless a manufacturing exemption applies), and other tangible assets would be subject to tax. The value of real estate and any land sold in connection with the transaction would not be subject to tax. In addition to a potential sales tax liability for the purchaser, the vendor may have some bulk sale reporting requirements in certain states.

Drop Shipments

Q 6:42 Do states tax drop shipments?

Yes. Absent a resale certificate or other specific exemption, all 45 states with a sales tax and the District of Columbia will tax drop shipments of retail sales of tangible personal property. The following 40 states and the District of Columbia require the supplier to receive a copy of the resale certificate from the vendor: Alabama, Arkansas, California, Colorado, Connecticut, Florida, Georgia, Hawaii, Illinois, Indiana, Kansas, Louisiana, Maine, Maryland, Massachusetts, Michigan, Minnesota, Mississippi, Missouri, Nebraska, Nevada, New Mexico, New York, North Carolina, North Dakota, Ohio, Oklahoma, Pennsylvania, Rhode Island, South Carolina, South Dakota, Tennessee, Texas, Utah, Vermont, Virginia, Washington, West Virginia, Wisconsin, and Wyoming. Of the 40 states requiring a resale certificate, 27 will accept either a multijurisdictional or the other state's resale license. These states are Alabama, Arizona, Arkansas, Colorado, Connecticut, Idaho, Illinois, Kentucky, Maine, Michigan, Minnesota, Missouri, Nebraska, New Jersey, New Mexico, New York, North Carolina, North Dakota, Ohio, Oklahoma, Pennsylvania, South Carolina, Texas, Utah, Virginia, West Virginia, and Wyoming. Arizona, Idaho, Kentucky, and Tennessee require some sort of documentation of a resale sale, but it need not be a license or resale certificate. Other states recently showing some flexibility on documentation include Missouri who will now accept a written resale exemption claim and Kansas. [*See* Mo. Dep't of Rev., Ltr. Rul. 1046 (issued May 30, 2002; expires May 30, 2005) and Kan. Dep't of Rev., Opinion Ltr. O-2002-014 (Aug. 15, 2002)]

Planning Point 6-27. In states that require the vendor to collect the tax for any drop shipments made on behalf of unregistered vendors, taxpayers are faced with a difficult dilemma. Because they are unregistered, they cannot provide an exemption certificate to the seller. This results in the sellers' being forced to bill the tax in order to protect themselves from additional assessment. The second seller is then forced to absorb the tax as a cost of doing business in the shipping destination state. In states like California, which have been aggressively enforcing drop shipment tax billing obligations, many vendors may find it advantageous to voluntarily register for use tax collection, even though they do not have nexus. By registering, they will be able to issue an exemption certificate and avoid being forced to absorb the tax on such transactions.

Pollution Control Equipment

Q 6:43 Do states exempt pollution control equipment from sales and use taxes?

Sixty percent of the states provide either reduced rates or complete exemption from sales and use tax for pollution control, waste treatment, or recycling equipment. Thirty-one states exempt pollution control equipment completely (Alabama, Arkansas, California (some), Connecticut, Georgia, Hawaii, Idaho, Illinois, Indiana, Iowa, Kansas, Kentucky, Louisiana, Maine, Maryland (only waste and sewerage pollution controls), Michigan, Minnesota (only purchases by steel-reprocessing firms), Mississippi (limited application after July 1, 2001), Missouri, New York, Ohio, Pennsylvania, Rhode Island, South Carolina, Tennessee, Texas (if useful life is less than six months), Utah, Virginia, Washington, West Virginia, and Wisconsin). Lower sales and use tax rates are imposed in North Carolina (1 percent, with maximum tax of $80 per item). Thirteen states and the District of Columbia do not provide any incentives or exemptions for tax on pollution control equipment (Arizona, Colorado, Florida,

Nebraska, Massachusetts, Nevada, New Jersey, New Mexico, North Dakota, Oklahoma, South Dakota, Vermont, and Wyoming). Because there is so much variation from state to state, special attention must be paid to each state's precise definition of qualifying equipment. Georgia, Ohio, Rhode Island, Virginia, and Wisconsin require that the pollution control equipment be properly certified by the appropriate state agency before the exemption will be allowed.

Planning Point 6-28. States that offer special exemptions for pollution control equipment commonly require that the purchaser obtain certification from the state department of natural resources or other body required to certify a pollution control facility. Taxpayers with purchases of this nature should be sure to check the specific registration requirements along with the appropriate procedure in the state of installation to avoid problems upon audit.

Construction Contractors

Q 6:50 What is the sales and use taxation of construction for exempt entities?

Most states provide statutory sales and use tax exemptions for sales to religious organizations, charitable groups, nonprofit educational institutions, and federal, state, and local governments. Generally, a religious, charitable, or nonprofit's sales tax exemption does not flow through to a contractor. The contractor must pay sales tax on the materials used in construction projects for exempt entities because it is the contractor, not the exempt entity, who is the end user of the tangible personal property. Consequently, in some states the sales tax can be avoided if the exempt entity purchases the materials itself. For example, the sales tax on materials used to build a church might be avoided if the church, rather than the contractor, purchased the building materials. In other states, statutory authority expressly authorizes the flow-through of exempt entities' status to the contractor's purchases.

Federal government. The exempt status of the federal government is extended to contractors in the following states: Alabama, Arizona (if an agency relationship exists), California, Colorado, Connecticut, Illinois, Kansas, Maine, Missouri, Nebraska (if supported by Form

17), New Jersey, New York, Ohio, Rhode Island, Texas (only on incorporated materials under a separate contract), Vermont, and the District of Columbia.

Religious organizations. The exempt status of a religious organization can be extended to contractors in Colorado, Connecticut, Illinois, Kansas, Maine, Maryland, Missouri, Nebraska (if supported by Form 17), New Jersey, New York, Ohio, Rhode Island, Texas (only on incorporated materials under a separate contract), Utah, Vermont, and the District of Columbia.

State and local governments. Only 15 states and the District of Columbia allow flow-through exemptions to the contractor for construction projects for state and local governments. The states include Alabama, Colorado, Connecticut, Illinois, Indiana, Kansas, Maine, Missouri (not state transportation), Nebraska (if supported by Form 17), New Jersey, New York, Ohio, Rhode Island, Texas, and Vermont (Vermont only).

Charities. The exempt status of qualifying charities is extended to contractors in the following states: Colorado, Connecticut, Illinois, Kansas, Maine, Maryland, New Jersey, New York, Ohio, Rhode Island, Texas, and Utah. If the charity or other qualifying not-for-profit group purchases the construction materials directly and contracts separately for their installation, the purchase will be exempt from sales tax in Arizona (some), Colorado, Connecticut, Florida, Illinois, Indiana, Kentucky, Maine, Maryland, Massachusetts, Minnesota, Missouri, Nebraska, Nevada, New Jersey, New York, Ohio, Oklahoma, Rhode Island, Utah, West Virginia, Wisconsin, and the District of Columbia.

Planning Point 6-33. A contractor should determine whether it will be subject to sales and use taxes before bidding on a project for an exempt organization. If the contractor fails to include a provision in the bid for use tax on the materials incorporated into the real estate of the exempt entity in a state that does not provide a flow-through of the exemption, the contractor may grossly understate the costs on the project and end up losing money on the contract. On the other hand, if the contractor includes tax on a bid that would be otherwise exempt, the contractor may lose the contract because its bid is too high. Multistate contractors must verify each state's treatment of the exemption flow-through to be certain that the proper taxes are paid.

Clothing

Q 6:59 Do the states impose their sales tax on clothing?

Yes, most states tax clothing. A few states provide for a taxable ceiling or floor; others exempt specific types of clothing. The following chart illustrates the tax status of clothing:

Taxability of Clothing

State	*Tax Status*
Alabama	Taxable
Arizona	Taxable
Arkansas	Taxable
California	Generally taxable
Colorado	Taxable
Connecticut	Exempts non-athletic clothing and footwear costing less than $75. Bicycle helmets and safety apparel are exempt.
District of Columbia	Taxable
Florida	Taxable
Georgia	Taxable
Hawaii	Taxable
Idaho	Generally taxable
Illinois	Taxable
Indiana	Generally taxable, except for qualifying safety clothing
Iowa	Taxable
Kansas	Taxable
Kentucky	Taxable
Louisiana	Taxable
Maine	Taxable
Maryland	Taxable
Massachusetts	Exempts non-athletic clothing and footwear costing less than $175
Michigan	Taxable
Minnesota	Generally exempt, except for athletic and recreational clothing
Mississippi	Taxable
Missouri	Taxable

State	*Tax Status*
Nebraska	Taxable
Nevada	Taxable
New Jersey	Generally exempts non-athletic clothing and footwear
New Mexico	Taxable
New York	Sales price of clothing and footwear up to $110 is exempt
North Carolina	Taxable
North Dakota	Taxable
Ohio	Taxable
Oklahoma	Taxable
Pennsylvania	Generally exempt, except for fur clothing, ornamental, formal, and athletic wear
Rhode Island	Exempts non-athletic clothing and footwear
South Carolina	Taxable
South Dakota	Taxable
Tennessee	Generally taxable, except for used clothing sales by nonprofit thrift shops
Texas	Generally taxable
Utah	Taxable
Vermont	Sales price of non-athletic clothing and footwear up to $110 is exempt
Virginia	Taxable
Washington	Generally taxable, except for display samples
West Virginia	Taxable
Wisconsin	Taxable
Wyoming	Taxable

Planning Point 6-38. Although sales of clothing are generally taxable, if the taxpayer can demonstrate that the clothing is required for product quality purposes and the state offers an exemption for items consumed or destroyed in the manufacturing process, then the item will usually be considered exempt. To demonstrate that clothing is required for product quality purposes, taxpayers must establish that direct contact with skin, perspiration, etc., would cause irreparable damage to the product being manufactured. Generally the types of clothing or apparel qualifying under this category include gloves, gowns, caps, finger cots or latex gloves, shoe covers, and similar items.

However, when clothing or wearing apparel is purchased for employee safety or appearance, the purchases are generally taxable. Even if there are OSHA requirements that forbid a company from requiring an employee to perform certain tasks without the safety attire, most states tax the items.

Planning Point 6-39. In recent years, states have adopted the practice of offering limited tax holidays on certain types of clothing. For example, a state may say that all children's clothing is nontaxable in the last two weeks of August. Although these holidays are helpful in stimulating sales and saving consumers money, they tend to be an enforcement problem for the states and a compliance problem for vendors. In short-term tax holidays such as these, computers must be reprogrammed for limited periods to avoid overtaxing the sales. In addition, many states only offer these holidays for a limited range of products. Therefore, there may be some similar items that are taxable, while other items are nontaxable during the holidays. For all these reasons, many groups are urging state legislatures to move away from this form of tax incentive.

Agricultural Equipment and Supplies

Q 6:62 Are agricultural chemicals, fertilizers, seeds, and feed subject to sales and use taxes?

No, most states do not tax agricultural chemicals, fertilizers, seeds, and feed. The exemption is based on the argument that these things should be exempt as resale sales because they become part of another product to be sold (crops, livestock, etc.). Using the same argument, a few states tax insecticides and pesticides on the grounds that their use is not to become part of the crop, per se, but to aid growth by protecting the crop from insects and pests. The following table illustrates the tax status of various agricultural items:

Sales Tax Status of Farm Chemicals, Fertilizer, Seeds, and Feed

State	*Insecticides and Pesticides*	*Fertilizer, Seed, and Feed*	*Seedlings Plants, and Shoots*
Alabama	Exempt	Exempt	Exempt
Arizona	Taxable	Exempt[1]	Exempt

State	*Insecticides and Pesticides*	*Fertilizer, Seed, and Feed*	*Seedlings Plants, and Shoots*
Arkansas	Exempt	Exempt	Exempt
California	Taxable	Exempt	Exempt
Colorado	Exempt	Exempt	Exempt
Connecticut	Exempt	Exempt	Exempt
District of Columbia	Taxable	Taxable	Taxable
Florida	Exempt	Exempt	Exempt
Georgia	Exempt	Exempt	Exempt
Hawaii[2]	Taxable	Taxable	Taxable
Idaho	Exempt	Exempt	Exempt
Illinois	Exempt	Exempt	Exempt
Indiana	Exempt	Exempt	Exempt
Iowa	Exempt	Exempt	Exempt
Kansas	Exempt	Exempt	Exempt
Kentucky	Exempt	Exempt	Exempt
Louisiana	Exempt	Exempt	Exempt
Maine	Exempt	Exempt	Exempt
Maryland	Exempt	Exempt	Exempt
Massachusetts	Exempt	Exempt	Exempt
Michigan	Exempt	Exempt	Exempt
Minnesota	Exempt	Exempt	Exempt
Mississippi	Exempt	Exempt	Exempt
Missouri	Exempt	Exempt	Exempt
Nebraska	Exempt	Exempt[3]	Exempt
Nevada	Taxable	Exempt	Exempt
New Jersey	Exempt	Exempt	Exempt
New Mexico	Exempt	Exempt	Exempt
New York	Exempt	Exempt	Exempt
North Carolina	Exempt	Exempt	Exempt
North Dakota	Exempt	Exempt	Exempt
Ohio	Exempt	Exempt	Exempt
Oklahoma	Exempt	Exempt	Exempt
Pennsylvania	Exempt	Exempt	Exempt
Rhode Island	Exempt	Exempt	Exempt
South Carolina	Exempt	Exempt	Exempt
South Dakota	Exempt	Exempt	Exempt
Tennessee	Exempt	Exempt	Exempt
Texas	Exempt	Exempt	Exempt

State	Insecticides and Pesticides	Fertilizer, Seed, and Feed	Seedlings Plants, and Shoots
Utah	Exempt	Exempt	Exempt
Vermont	Exempt	Exempt	Exempt
Virginia	Exempt	Exempt	Exempt
Washington	Exempt	Exempt	Exempt
West Virginia	Exempt	Exempt	Exempt
Wisconsin	Exempt	Exempt	Exempt
Wyoming	Exempt	Exempt	Exempt

[1] Feed exemption only.
[2] Taxed at wholesale rate.
[3] Commercial fertilizers are taxable.

Business-Related Expenses of Government Employees

Q 6:64 Do states impose their sales tax on purchases of business-related expenses by federal government employees?

States will impose sales tax on purchases of business-related expenses by federal government employees unless the purchase is paid directly by the federal government either through an official purchase order, a government credit card, or direct billing. Purchases made by a federal employee for which she will be reimbursed are taxable. It does not matter whether the purchase is made through a travel advance or even on a credit card stamped with the government agency's name. The payment must be made directly by the federal government and not through any intermediary. For example, a federal employee travels from Washington, D.C., to Cheyenne, Wyoming, for meetings with the local Environmental Protection Administration (EPA) office. She charges her airfare, lodging, and meals to her EPA-issued credit card. The federal employee is responsible for paying the credit card bill and turning in her receipts for reimbursement. Her charges and payments are not exempt from sales tax. If the bill for the card was paid directly by the federal government the purchases are exempt from sales tax.

The federal government issues four different types of charge cards to its employees under a credit card program called "GSA SmartPay." The four cards are as follows:

Fleet card. Purchases made with Fleet cards are nontaxable. The Fleet card displays a picture of cars. Purchases are billed directly to the federal government agency.

Purchasing card. Purchases with the Purchasing card are nontaxable. The Purchasing card displays a picture of the U.S. Capitol. Purchases are billed directly to the federal government agency.

Integrated card and *travel card.* These two cards may be billed either to the individual carrying the card or directly to the federal government. The sixth digit on the card indicates whether the purchase is paid directly by the federal government or by the individual. If the sixth digit is a 1, 2, 3, or 4, the individual is being billed and the purchase is taxable. If the sixth digit is a 0, 6, 7, 8, or 9, the federal government agency is being billed and the purchase will be exempt from sales tax.

The Supremacy Clause of the U.S. Constitution prohibits states from directly taxing sales to the federal government. Chief Justice John Marshall ruled in *McCulloch v. Maryland,* 17 U.S. 316 (1819), that a state tax directly imposed on the federal government or its instrumentalities was an unconstitutional violation of the Supremacy Clause. (For a detailed discussion of the Supremacy Clause, see chapter 6 of the State and Local Taxation Answer Book by James T. Collins and Robert M. Kozub (Panel Publishers 2000).)

The following table summarizes the state application of sales tax to federal government employees' travel expenses.

State Sales Taxation of Federal Government Employees' Travel Expenses

Item	*Tax Status*	*States*
Direct-billed	Taxable	South Carolina
Purchase of a product	Exempt	In all states except for South Carolina
Employee-paid and reimbursed purchase of a product	Taxable	In all states except for Florida, Missouri
	Exempt	Florida, Missouri

Item	*Tax Status*	*States*
Direct-billed purchase of a service	Taxable	Hawaii, Massachusetts, New Mexico, South Carolina
	Exempt	In all states except Hawaii, Massachusetts, New Mexico, South Carolina
Employee-paid and reimbursed purchase of a service	Taxable	Arkansas, California, Connecticut, District of Columbia, Florida, Georgia, Hawaii, Idaho, Illinois, Iowa, Kansas, Kentucky, Louisiana, Maine, Maryland, Michigan, Minnesota, Mississippi, Nebraska, New Jersey, New Mexico, New York, North Dakota, Ohio, Pennsylvania, Rhode Island, South Carolina, South Dakota, Tennessee, Texas (unless the employee provides a certificate to the seller), Utah, Vermont, Washington, West Virginia, Wisconsin, Wyoming
	Exempt	Alabama, Arizona, Colorado, Florida, Indiana, Massachusetts, Missouri, Nevada, North Carolina, Oklahoma, Virginia
Direct-billed hotel/motel charges	Taxable	Arizona, Hawaii, Massachusetts, New Mexico, South Carolina
	Exempt	In all states except for Arizona, Hawaii, Massachusetts, New Mexico, South Carolina
Employee-paid and reimbursed hotel/motel charges	Taxable	In all states except for Florida, Louisiana, Missouri, Nevada, New York, Pennsylvania, Texas
	Exempt	Florida, Louisiana, Missouri, Nevada, New York (must provide an exemption certificate), Pennsylvania, Texas

Q 6:65 Do states tax purchases of business-related expenses by state government employees?

Most states exempt business-related expenses by state and local government employees from sales tax if the purchase is paid directly by the state or local government either through an official purchase order, a government credit card, or direct billing. The exemption does not usually extend to other states or their local political jurisdictions. Purchases made by a state or local government employee for which she will be reimbursed are taxable. It does not matter whether the purchase is made through a travel advance or even on a credit card stamped with the government agency's name. The payment must be made directly by the state and local government and not through any intermediary. For example, a city employee travels from Dallas to Houston for meetings with other city officials from around the state. She charges her gas, lodging, and meals to her city-issued credit card. The city employee is responsible for paying the credit card bill and turning in her receipts for reimbursement. Her charges and payments are not exempt from sales tax. If the card was a direct-pay charge card, which means the city government is billed, the purchases are exempt from sales tax. Direct-pay charge cards issued by state and local governments are usually identified by specific language such as, "For Official State Business Only" or "State Tax Exempt."

The following table summarizes state sales tax treatment of a state employee's travel expenses.

State Sales Taxation of State Employees' Travel Expenses

Item	*Tax Status*	*States*
Direct-billed purchase of a product	Taxable	Arizona, Arkansas, California, District of Columbia, Hawaii, North Carolina (except the North Carolina Department of Transportation), Pennsylvania, Washington
	Exempt	Alabama, Colorado, Connecticut, Florida, Georgia, Idaho, Illinois, Indiana, Iowa, Kansas, Kentucky, Louisiana, Maine, Maryland, Massachusetts, Michigan, Minnesota (exceptions exist), Mississippi, Missouri, Nebraska, Nevada, New Jersey, New Mexico, New York, North Dakota, Ohio, Oklahoma, Rhode Island, South Carolina, South Dakota, Tennessee (credit cards representing direct billing to the governmental unit are tax-exempt), Texas, Utah, Vermont, Virginia, West Virginia, Wisconsin, Wyoming

Item	*Tax Status*	*States*
Employee-paid and reimbursed purchase of a product	Taxable	In all states except Massachusetts and Missouri
	Exempt	Massachusetts, Missouri
Direct-billed purchase of a service	Taxable	Arkansas, District of Columbia, Hawaii, Minnesota, New Mexico, Pennsylvania, Washington
	Exempt	In all states except Arkansas, Hawaii, Minnesota, New Mexico, Pennsylvania, Washington, and the District of Columbia
Employee-paid and reimbursed purchase of a service	Taxable	Arkansas, Connecticut, District of Columbia, Florida, Georgia, Hawaii, Idaho, Illinois, Iowa, Kansas, Kentucky, Louisiana, Maine, Maryland, Michigan, Minnesota, Mississippi, Nebraska, New Jersey, New Mexico, New York, North Dakota, Ohio, Pennsylvania, Rhode Island, South Carolina, South Dakota, Tennessee, Texas (unless the employee provides a certificate to the seller), Utah, Vermont, Washington, West Virginia, Wisconsin, Wyoming
	Exempt	Alabama, Arizona, California, Colorado, Indiana, Massachusetts, Missouri, Nevada, North Carolina, Oklahoma, Virginia
Direct-billed hotel/motel charges	Taxable	Alabama (subject to the lodging tax), Arizona, Arkansas, Hawaii, Massachusetts, Minnesota, New Mexico, North Carolina (except for the North Carolina Department of Transportation), Pennsylvania, Virginia, Washington
	Exempt	California, Colorado, Connecticut, District of Columbia, Florida, Georgia, Idaho, Illinois, Indiana, Iowa, Kansas, Kentucky, Louisiana, Maine, Maryland, Michigan, Mississippi, Missouri,

Item	*Tax Status*	*States*
		Nebraska, Nevada, New Jersey, New York, North Dakota, Ohio, Oklahoma, Rhode Island, South Carolina, South Dakota, Tennessee, Texas, Utah, Vermont, West Virginia, Wisconsin, Wyoming
Employee-paid and reimbursed hotel/motel charges	Taxable	Alabama, Arizona, Arkansas, Colorado, Connecticut, District of Columbia, Florida, Georgia, Hawaii, Idaho, Illinois, Indiana, Iowa, Kansas, Kentucky, Maine, Maryland, Massachusetts, Michigan, Minnesota, Mississippi, Nebraska, New Jersey, New Mexico, North Carolina, North Dakota, Ohio, Oklahoma, Pennsylvania, Rhode Island, South Carolina, South Dakota, Tennessee (credit cards representing direct billing to government are tax-exempt), Utah, Vermont, Washington, West Virginia, Wisconsin, Wyoming
	Exempt	California, Louisiana, Missouri, Nevada, New York, Texas

Food and Beverages

Q 6:66 Are sales of food and beverages subject to sales and use taxes?

The answer to the question depends on how food and beverages are classified. For example, about two-thirds of the states exempt unprepared food purchased in grocery stores. Prepared foods and food for immediate consumption are taxable in every state. The following chart summarizes the sales and use tax treatment of food and beverages (except for vending machines) in the various states.

Planning Point 6-40. The treatment of a gratuity in a restaurant can vary in some states, depending on whether it is a voluntary or mandatory contribution. When large groups eat in restaurants, the establishment may automatically add 15 to 20 percent to the bill in the form of a mandatory minimum tip. Many states treat that charge as an additional cost for the food that is subject to tax. On the other hand, if the patron voluntarily offers a 15 to 20 percent tip, the charge is not subject to tax. Taxpayers holding large meetings or banquets for employees and guests should carefully check their restaurant bills to make sure that the gratuity charge is being properly handled for sales and use tax purposes.

Sales Tax Status of Food and Beverages

Tax Status	*States*
	Unprepared Food from a Grocery Store
Taxable	Alabama, Arkansas, Hawaii, Idaho, Illinois (taxable at a reduced rate), Kansas, Louisiana (taxable at a reduced rate), Mississippi, Missouri, New Mexico, North Carolina, Oklahoma, South Carolina, South Dakota, Tennessee, Utah, Virginia, West Virginia, Wyoming
Exempt	Arizona, California, Colorado, Connecticut (snack food excluded from the exemption), District of Columbia, Florida, Georgia, Indiana, Iowa, Kentucky, Maine (snack food excluded from the exemption), Maryland, Massachusetts, Michigan, Minnesota, Missouri, Nebraska, Nevada, New Jersey, New York, New York City, North Dakota, Ohio, Pennsylvania, Rhode Island, Texas, Vermont, Washington, Wisconsin (some snack food excluded from the exemption)
	Sales of Prepared Foods
Taxable	In all states except Vermont
Exempt	Vermont (if subject to meals and room tax)
	Food Prepared by Caterers
Taxable	In all states except Vermont
Exempt	Vermont (if subject to meals and room tax)
	Beverages
Taxable	In all states other than those exceptions listed below
Exempt	Minnesota (for milk and beverages containing 50% or

Tax Status	*States*
	more fruit juice), New York (for beverages other than alcoholic beverages, soft drinks, and fruit juices), New York City (same as New York State)
	Water
Taxable	Alabama, Arizona (if bottled), Arkansas, California (if carbonated or effervescent), Colorado, Connecticut (if bottled), Georgia, Hawaii, Idaho (if bottled), Illinois (if bottled), Indiana, Iowa, Kansas, Kentucky, Louisiana, Maine (except for sales for residential premises), Maryland (if bottled), Minnesota (if sold commercially, if carbonated, and if bottled waters in containers less than one half of a gallon), Mississippi (if bottled), Missouri, Nebraska, New Mexico, New York (exempt if delivered through pipes or mains), New York City (exempt if delivered through pipes or mains), North Carolina (bottled water only), North Dakota (unless sold in quantities greater than one gallon), Ohio (bottled water only), Oklahoma, Pennsylvania (if bottled or flavored), Rhode Island, South Carolina, Tennessee, Utah, Virginia, Washington (bottled water), West Virginia (if purchased from a retailer), Wyoming
Exempt	Florida (unless carbonated or flavored), Massachusetts, Michigan, Nevada, New Jersey, South Dakota, Texas, Vermont, Wisconsin
	Soft Drinks
Taxable	In all states with a sales tax except for Vermont (if subject to the meals and room tax)

Fuel

Q 6:69 How are fuels used in the production process treated for sales and use tax purposes?

The majority of the states with a manufacturing exemption exempt fuels used in the production process from sales and use taxation.

Sales and Use Taxation of Fuels Used in the Production Process

Tax Status	*States*
Taxable	Arizona, Arkansas (exemptions for natural gas and electricity sold to certain steel mills, electricity used in certain aluminum processes, natural gas used in manufacturing glass, and waste fuel used in manufacturing), California (some exceptions exist and partial exemptions allowed for start-up companies), Georgia (exemption for electricity used in production), Hawaii, Illinois, Louisiana, Maine, Mississippi (reduced rate available), Nevada, New Mexico, New Jersey, North Carolina, North Dakota, Oklahoma, South Dakota, Washington, Wisconsin (a limited exemption is available for wood used as fuel; a franchise tax credit for the tax paid on fuel used in manufacturing)
Exempt	Alabama, Colorado, Connecticut, District of Columbia, Florida, Idaho, Indiana, Iowa, Kansas, Kentucky, Maryland, Massachusetts, Michigan, Minnesota, Missouri, Nebraska, New York, New York City, Ohio, Pennsylvania, Rhode Island, South Carolina, Tennessee (or reduced rate), Texas, Utah, Vermont, Virginia, West Virginia (the exemption is not available to gasoline and special fuels), Wyoming

Medicines and Medical Supplies

Q 6:74 Are medicines and medical devices subject to sales tax?

All but two states (Hawaii and Illinois) exempt prescription medicine from sales and use tax. All but nine states and the District of Columbia tax nonprescription medicine (Connecticut, Florida, Maryland, New Jersey, New York, Pennsylvania, Rhode Island, Texas, and Vermont). Most states require that the prescription be written by a licensed physician, but a few states accept prescriptions written by any licensed health care provider. Other common medical sales and use tax exemptions include insulin, insulin measuring and injecting devices (syringes and needles), glucose, urine- and blood-testing kits.

Diet foods and vitamins are usually subject to tax although there are exceptions. New York recently issued a ruling exempting certain dietary food supplements and antiseptic burn medicine for treatment against infections. [N.Y. Dep't of Tax'n, TSB-A-02(36)S July 25, 2002)] Kansas exempts the sale of human skin used in skin grafts. [Kan. Dep't of Rev., Ltr. Rul. P-2002-068 (Aug. 15, 2002)] Most states have not specifically addressed whether or not the sale of blood is a taxable transaction. As tangible personal property, it would generally be deemed taxable and so a Tennessee court has held. [*See* Parkridge Hospital v. Woods, 561 S.W.2d 754 (Tenn. 1978)]

All but seven states exempt prosthetic devices. Prosthetic devices are artificial parts that aid or replace a body part or function, although the precise scope of the definition varies from state to state. For example, some states require that to be a qualifying prosthetic device, it must be designed, manufactured, or adjusted to fit one individual. In those states, one-size-fits-all items such as crutches, walkers, and canes would not qualify as prosthetic devices. However, the California State Board of Equalization recently held that continuous passive motion machines used in rehabilitation qualify as exempt orthopedic devices even where the device is not worn on the body. [*In re* Action Medical Products, Inc., No. 57424 (Cal. St. Bd. of Equal. Apr. 18, 2002)] The items most often challenged with respect to prosthetic devices include hearing aids, orthodontic work, eyeglasses, orthopedic devices, and contact lenses.

An issue closely related to the exempt status of medicine and medical devices is whether the transfer of medical records for a fee is subject to sales or use tax. The answer depends upon whether the state views the transfer as one of tangible personal property or a nontaxable service. State courts are split on this issue with taxpayers usually victorious if they can convince the court that the true object of the transaction is the acquisition of information and provision of a service, not the hard-copy records themselves. The Kentucky Court of Appeals recently ruled that providing copies of medical records to a law firm for a fee was not the exercising of a taxable privilege, but the discharging of a medical duty required by state statute. [Woodward, Hobson, & Fulton, LLP v. Revenue Cabinet, 69 S.W.3d 476 (Ky. Ct. App. 2002)]

The following chart summarizes the sales and use tax treatment of medicines and medical devices.

Sales Tax Treatment of Medicines and Medical Devices

State	*Prescription Medicines*	*Nonprescription Medicines*	*Prosthetic Devices*
Alabama	Exempt	Taxable	Taxable
Arizona	Exempt	Taxable	Exempt[1]
Arkansas	Exempt	Taxable	Exempt[1]
California	Exempt	Taxable	Exempt[1]
Colorado	Exempt	Taxable	Exempt
Connecticut	Exempt	Exempt	Exempt
District of Columbia	Exempt	Exempt	Exempt
Florida	Exempt	Exempt	Exempt
Georgia	Exempt	Taxable	Taxable[2]
Hawaii	Taxable	Taxable	Exempt[1]
Idaho	Exempt	Taxable	Exempt
Illinois	Taxable[3,4,5]	Taxable[3,4,5]	Taxable[3,4,5]
Indiana	Exempt	Taxable	Exempt[1]
Iowa	Exempt	Taxable	Exempt
Kansas	Exempt	Taxable[6]	Exempt[1]
Kentucky	Exempt	Taxable	Exempt[1]
Louisiana	Exempt	Taxable	Exempt[1]
Maine	Exempt	Taxable	Exempt
Maryland	Exempt	Exempt	Exempt
Massachusetts	Exempt	Taxable	Exempt[1]
Michigan	Exempt	Taxable	Exempt[1]
Minnesota	Exempt	Taxable[7]	Exempt
Mississippi	Exempt	Taxable	Taxable
Missouri	Exempt	Taxable	Exempt
Nebraska	Exempt	Taxable	Exempt[1]
Nevada	Exempt	Taxable	Exempt
New Jersey	Exempt	Exempt	Exempt
New Mexico	Exempt	Taxable	Taxable[8]
New York	Exempt	Exempt	Exempt
North Carolina	Exempt	Taxable	Exempt[1]
North Dakota	Exempt	Taxable	Exempt
Ohio	Exempt	Taxable	Exempt
Oklahoma	Exempt	Taxable	Taxable[9]
Pennsylvania	Exempt	Exempt	Exempt
Rhode Island	Exempt	Exempt	Exempt
South Carolina	Exempt	Taxable	Exempt[1]
South Dakota	Exempt	Taxable	Exempt[1]
Tennessee	Exempt	Taxable	Exempt

State	*Prescription Medicines*	*Nonprescription Medicines*	*Prosthetic Devices*
Texas	Exempt	Exempt	Exempt
Utah	Exempt	Taxable	Taxable
Vermont	Exempt	Exempt	Exempt[1]
Virginia	Exempt	Taxable	Exempt
Washington	Exempt	Taxable	Exempt[1]
West Virginia	Exempt	Taxable	Exempt
Wisconsin	Exempt	Taxable	Exempt
Wyoming	Exempt	Taxable	Exempt

[1] Exempt if prescribed by a person authorized by law.

[2] Prosthetic devices are exempt when paid for directly by state or federal funds under Medicare or Medicaid programs when state or federal law or regulation prohibits the payment of sales and use tax.

[3] Subject to a reduced rate of tax.

[4] Exempt from Use Tax, Retailer's Occupation Tax, Service Occupation Tax, and Service Use Tax when sold by certain not-for-profit organizations.

[5] Exempt from Service Occupation Tax when purchased for use by a person receiving medical assistance and who resides in a licensed long-term care facility.

[6] Sales to nonprofit skilled nursing homes or nonprofit intermediate care nursing homes are exempt.

[7] Painkillers consisting mainly of acetaminophen, acetylsalicylic acid, and ibuprofen are exempt.

[8] Deductible from gross receipts when sold to a licensed medical practitioner who delivers the device incidental to a service and includes the value of the device in the service charge.

[9] Exempt when reimbursed under Medicare or Medicaid.

Newspapers and Publications

Q 6:75 Are newspapers and periodicals subject to sales tax?

It is difficult to find state consistency in the sales and use taxation of newspapers, magazines, and periodicals. The reasons for differences in treatment include specific exemptions and differences in classification. In some states, the sale of newspapers is the sale of tangible personal property and is taxable. In other states, the sale of newspapers is the sale of a nontaxable service. Some states tax magazines but not newspapers, others tax newsletters but not newspapers. [*See* Magazine Publishers of Am. v. Department of Rev., 654 A.2d 519 (Pa. 1995) and Bancroft Info. Group v. Comptroller, 603 A.2d 1289 (Md. 1992)] The sales and use tax exemptions for machinery and equipment used in manufacturing may be available to newspaper and magazine publishers in those states that treat the sales of newspapers and magazines as sales of tangible personal property.

State treatment of newspapers and periodicals has received significant judicial scrutiny of late with respect to the application of specific exemptions. Although the courts have allowed states "broad latitude in creating classifications and distinctions in tax statutes," distinctions based on content will not be allowed. [Leathers v. Medlock, 499 U.S. 439, 451 (1991) (quoting Regan v. Taxation with Representation of Wash., 461 U.S. 540, 547 (1983)] Thus, different tax treatment is permitted between newspapers, newsletters, and magazines, but sales tax exemptions limited to only Bibles or other religious periodicals are a violation of the First Amendment's prohibition against establishment of religion. [Ahlburn v. Clark, 728 A.2d 449 (R.I. 1999) and Texas Monthly v. Bullock, 489 U.S. 1 (1989)]

The following chart summarizes the sales tax status of newspapers, magazines, and other periodicals.

State Sales Taxation of Newspapers and Periodicals

State	*Newspapers*	*Periodicals*
Alabama	Taxable	Taxable
Arizona	Taxable	Taxable
Arkansas	Exempt	Taxable[1]
California	Taxable[2]	Taxable[2]
Colorado	Exempt	Taxable
Connecticut	Exempt	Taxable
District of Columbia	Taxable[3]	Taxable
Florida	Taxable	Taxable
Georgia	Taxable	Taxable
Hawaii	Taxable	Taxable
Idaho	Taxable	Taxable
Illinois	Exempt	Exempt
Indiana	Exempt	Taxable
Iowa	Exempt	Taxable
Kansas	Taxable	Taxable
Kentucky	Taxable	Taxable
Louisiana	Taxable	Taxable
Maine	Exempt	Exempt
Maryland	Taxable[3]	Taxable
Massachusetts	Exempt	Exempt
Michigan	Exempt[3]	Exempt[3]

State	*Newspapers*	*Periodicals*
Minnesota	Exempt	Taxable[1]
Mississippi	Exempt	Exempt
Missouri	Taxable	Taxable
Nebraska	Exempt[4]	Exempt[4]
Nevada	Exempt	Taxable
New Jersey	Exempt	Exempt[5]
New Mexico	Exempt	Taxable
New York	Exempt	Exempt
North Carolina	Exempt[6]	Exempt[6]
North Dakota	Exempt	Taxable
Ohio	Exempt	Exempt[7]
Oklahoma	Exempt	Exempt
Pennsylvania	Exempt	Taxable[8]
Rhode Island	Exempt	Taxable
South Carolina	Exempt	Taxable
South Dakota	Taxable	Taxable
Tennessee	Exempt	Exempt[1]
Texas	Exempt[9]	Taxable
Utah	Exempt	Taxable
Vermont	Exempt	Taxable
Virginia	Exempt[10]	Exempt[10]
Washington	Exempt	Taxable
West Virginia	Exempt[11]	Taxable
Wisconsin	Exempt	Exempt[8]
Wyoming	Exempt	Taxable[8]

[1] Magazines and periodicals are exempt from sales taxation if sold by subscription.

[2] Newspapers, magazines, and periodical subscriptions are exempt from sales and use tax if issued at least every four months or 60 times a year and delivered by mail or common carrier.

[3] Newspapers, magazines, and periodicals are exempt if they are sent second-class mail or they are a controlled circulation publication or are qualified to accept legal notices, or have been in existence for two years or more and have been published at least once a week.

[4] Newspapers issued at least once a week are exempt. Monthly magazines and journals are exempt if purchased by subscription.

[5] Magazines and periodicals are exempt if issued at least four times a year.

[6] This exemption applies only to newspapers and magazines sold by street vendors and door-to-door vendors.

[7] Magazines and periodicals are exempt if they are sold by subscription and shipped by second-class mail or the magazines are distributed under controlled circulation.

[8] If sold by subscription.

[9] Newspapers are exempt if the average sales price does not exceed 75 cents. Subscriptions to magazines are exempt if sold for a six-month or longer period and the magazines are delivered by second-class mail.

[10] Newsstand sales are taxable.

[11] Exempt if delivered by route carriers.

Planning Point 6-44. Generally, to be considered a periodical, publications must be issued at regular intervals, not exceeding three or six months and be the type of publication that is available for reading by the general public. Therefore, publications by special interest groups that are offered as part of a membership in an organization frequently will not qualify.

Utilities

Q 6:76 Is electricity subject to the sales and use tax?

Yes. Most states report that they levy sales and use tax on the purchase or consumption of electricity. However, some states exempt residential use, others exempt electricity used in manufacturing or other industrial uses. In a rather unusual decision, the Missouri Supreme Court ruled that the sale of electricity to a Hyatt hotel was exempt from sales tax as a sale for resale. The exemption only applied to electricity used in hotel, meeting, and banquet rooms let to the public by Hyatt for a fee or room rental. [Kansas City Power and Light Co. v. Dir. of Rev., No. SC84117 (Mo. Sup. Ct. July 23, 2002)] The following table indicates the tax status of electrical power.

State Sales and Use Tax Treatment of Electrical Power

Tax Treatment	*States*
Taxable	Arizona, Arkansas, Colorado (but exempt for residential use), Connecticut, District of Columbia, Florida (but exempt for residential use), Georgia, Hawaii, Indiana, Iowa, Kansas, Kentucky (but exempt for residential use), Louisiana, Maine, Maryland, Massachusetts, Michigan, Minnesota, Mississippi (but exempt for residential use), Missouri, Nebraska, New Jersey, New Mexico (if other fuel taxes were not paid), New York (commercial uses only), New York City (commercial uses only), North Carolina, Ohio (if obtained from sources other than a public utility), Oklahoma, Pennsylvania (commercial uses only), Rhode Island, South Carolina (with exemptions), South Dakota, Ten-

Tax Treatment	*States*
	nessee, Texas, Utah, Vermont (substantial exceptions exist), Wisconsin, Wyoming
Exempt	Alabama, California, Idaho, Illinois, Nevada, North Dakota, Virginia, Washington, West Virginia

Planning Point 6-45. With the deregulation of electricity and other energy sources, taxpayers have a new area of exposure for sales and use taxes. In the past, taxpayers purchased energy from their local utility and they could count on the local utility to serve as a tax collector for the state. With deregulation, taxpayers may be dealing with vendors that are located outside the state and that lack the necessary presence in the state to trigger nexus. Consequently, these vendors are not required to bill the tax and generally do not. Taxpayers purchasing electricity and other energy sources from outside their state should make sure they establish procedures to correctly self-assess use tax on these purchases.

Prepaid Phone Cards

Q 6:78 Are prepaid phone calls subject to sales and use taxes?

Prepaid phone cards (PPC) illustrate some of the problems presented by the growth in high technology and e-commerce. PPCs generally fall into one of three categories and can be purchased in either units of time (minutes) or dollar denominations. The first category of PPC is your typical standard PPC that can be purchased anywhere from convenience stores to vending machines. Next, there are promotional PPCs embossed with a vendor's name or product and either packaged with other products or given away by the vendor to customers as part of an advertising or promotional campaign. Finally, some PPCs are issued as plastic collectibles stamped with the color picture of some person, place, or thing. The value of collectible PPCs is not tied to the telephone service it represents, but can vary depending on the embossed image, the number issued, and whether it has remained unsealed and unused. Whether standard, promotional, or collector issued, every PPC allows the purchaser to make phone calls via "800" numbers. The calls are identified, routed, and tracked such that the purchaser's units (either time or dollars) can be appropriately charged.

The invention and widespread use of PPCs has raised several questions regarding how they should be taxed, if at all, for sales and use taxes. First, is the sale of a PPC a sale of tangible personal property or the sale of a telecommunications service? If it is the sale of a telecommunications service, where should the calls be sourced, who should collect and remit the tax, and what is the tax base: the sales price of the card, or the value of the telecommunications service embedded in the card? State answers to these questions vary, have changed over time, and continue to evolve.

The sales and use taxation of prepaid phone cards is described in the table below.

Sales and Use Taxation of Prepaid Phone Cards

Tax Status	*States*
Taxed as telecommunications services when used by the consumer	California, Colorado (if the value of the phone services are stated in terms of minutes of service), Georgia, Massachusetts, South Carolina, Wisconsin
Sale of prepaid phone cards taxed as the sale of tangible personal property at the point of sale	Alabama, Arizona, Arkansas, Colorado (if the value of the phone services are stated in terms of dollars), Connecticut, District of Columbia, Florida, Hawaii, Idaho (only if sold as a collectible item), Iowa, Kansas, Kentucky, Louisiana, Maine, Maryland, Michigan, Minnesota, Mississippi, Missouri, Nebraska, New Jersey, New Mexico, North Dakota, Ohio, Oklahoma, Pennsylvania, Rhode Island, South Dakota, Tennessee, Texas, Utah, Washington, West Virginia, Wyoming
The retail purchase and later use of the card subject to tax as both the sale of telecommunications services and the sale of tangible personal property	Indiana, Rhode Island
Not taxed	Nevada, Virginia

Q 6:79 How are prepaid phone calls taxed as telecommunications services?

The U.S. Supreme Court has upheld the right of a state to tax an *interstate* phone call if the call either originated or terminated in the state and was billed to an address in the state. [Goldberg v. Sweet, 488 U.S. 252 (1989)] The *Goldberg* two-out-of-three test (origination, termination, and billing address) sets the standard against which a state's telecommunication sales tax rules are judged. Debate continues about the specific application of the *Goldberg* test to PPCs because the billing address part of the test is inapplicable. Consequently, states are left with one of five options in taxing PPCs. They may tax (1) calls that originate in the customer's state; (2) calls that terminate in the customer's state; (3) calls that *both* originate and terminate in the customer's state; (4) calls that *either* originate or terminate in the customer's state; or finally, (5) the sale of the PPC itself.

How PPCs Are Taxed

Tax Status	*States*
Calls originating in the customer's state	Florida (if billed in state), Massachusetts, Ohio
Calls terminating in the customer's state	Connecticut, Florida (if billed in state)
Calls that both originate and terminate in the customer's state	California, Georgia, Kentucky, North Carolina, Ohio
Calls that originate or terminate in the customer's state	None
Taxed where the PPC is purchased	Utah, Wisconsin

Q 6:80 When PPCs are taxed as telecommunications services, who is liable for remitting the tax?

The responsibility for remitting the tax may lie with (1) whoever sells the PPC at retail; (2) whoever sells the PPC at wholesale; or (3) the telecommunications service provider.

Liability for Remitting the Telecommunications Tax

Party	*States*
PPC retailer	Illinois (Telecommunications Excise Tax), Utah, Wisconsin
PPC wholesaler	None
Telecommunications service provider	California, Colorado, Georgia, Kentucky, Massachusetts, North Carolina, Ohio, South Carolina

Procurement Cards

Q 6:85 If a procurement or debit card is used, when is the sale deemed to be made for sales tax purposes?

There are four possibilities: (1) at the time of the charge; (2) on the date the tangible personal property was shipped or the services were rendered; (3) when payment is made to the credit card company; or (4) some other designated date. The problem for taxpayers is that with monthly billings it may be difficult to file timely for purchases where the tax accrues at the time the card is charged.

States' Treatment of the Purchase/Sale Date

Date	*States*
At the time of the charge	Arkansas, Connecticut, District of Columbia, Florida, Idaho, Kansas, Kentucky, Maryland, Massachusetts, Mississippi, Missouri, New Jersey, North Carolina, Ohio, Oklahoma, Pennsylvania, South Dakota, Vermont, Virginia, Washington
Date the goods were transferred or the services were rendered	Arizona, California, Colorado, Hawaii, Indiana, Iowa, Louisiana, Maine, Michigan, Nebraska, Nevada, New York, North Dakota, Rhode Island, South Carolina, Texas, Utah, West Virginia, Wisconsin, Wyoming
Time of payment to the credit card company	Georgia
Other	Alabama (when title passes), Illinois (when title passes), Minnesota (when title passes)

Tax on Services

Q 6:88 What states levy sales and use taxes on services?

While Hawaii, New Mexico, and South Dakota tax almost all services, most states tax only a few enumerated services. These states and the services they tax are listed in the following table.

State	*Taxable Services*
Alabama	Amusement admissions
Arizona	Amusement admissions; job printing; prime contracting; publication; restaurants; telecommunications; lodging; utilities; transportation
Arkansas	Utilities; telephone and telecommunications; lodging; cleaning; printing; photography; cable television; amusement admissions
California	Does not generally tax services
Colorado	Telecommunications; gas, electric, and steam services; service of food or drink; furnishing accommodations
Connecticut	Advertising and public relations; amusements; business analysis, management, and management consulting; community antenna television services; computer and data processing; credit information and reporting; employment and personnel agency; extermination; flight instruction and chartering; furniture repair and reupholstering; janitorial services; landscaping; lobbying; locksmith services; maintenance; motor vehicle parking and washing; painting and lettering; personal services under SIC group 729; photographic services; private investigation, patrol, and protection; renovation and repair; service in connection with the sale of tangible personal property; piped-in music; service to industrial, commercial, or income-producing real property; stenography; swimming pool cleaning and maintenance; tax preparation; telecommunications; telephone answering; window cleaning
District of Columbia	Vending machines; real property maintenance services; landscaping services; data pro-

State	*Taxable Services*
	cessing; information services; amusement admissions; telecommunications; laundry; delivery; accommodations
Florida	Amusement admissions; telecommunications, transportation and public utilities
Georgia	Utilities; amusement admissions; accommodations
Hawaii	Virtually all services
Idaho	Printing; providing food or drink; accommodations; leasing tangible personal property; intrastate transportation; recreational admissions
Illinois	Service Occupation Tax is imposed on the selling price of the tangible personal property transferred incidental to the services
Indiana	Water softening and conditioning; accommodations; electrical energy, natural or artificial gas; water, steam, or steam heat; telephone or telecommunications; intra-state telegraph; leasing of tangible personal property; intrastate cable television
Iowa	Admissions; gas, electric, water, heat; pay television, or communication services; engraving, photography, printing, or binding; vulcanizing, recapping and retreading services; optional service or warranty; transient lodging; solid waste collection and disposal
Kansas	Admissions; dues; gas, water, electricity, and heat; coin-operated devices; computer software services; dry cleaning and laundry; transient lodging; installation and application services if property is not held for sale in the normal course of business; interstate and intrastate telephone and telegraph services; furnishing meals or drinks; radio and television subscription services; repair, service alternation, or maintenance of tangible personal property; leasing of tangible personal property; telecommunications; vehicle washing services
Kentucky	Rental of transient accommodations; furnishing of sewer services; intrastate telephone and telegraph; admissions

State	Taxable Services
Louisiana	Providing lodging; telecommunications; parking; admissions; printing; cleaning; cold storage; repair
Maine	Rental of lodging; rental of autos; telephone or telegraph; extended cable television; custom computer programming; rental of videotapes, equipment, and furniture; electricity
Maryland	Fabricating, printing, or production of tangible personal property; commercial cleaning or laundering; telecommunications services; pay-per-view television; credit reporting; security services; janitorial services; gas and electric utilities
Massachusetts	Utilities; telecommunications; certain printing and fabrication services
Michigan	Telecommunications; providing lodging
Minnesota	Providing meals; admissions and membership fees; providing lodging; utilities; telecommunications; parking; cleaning; security services; pet and lawn care
Mississippi	Air conditioning installation and repairs; repairs of motor vehicles; amusements; security services; car washing; and 40 other specific services
Missouri	Utilities; telecommunications; furnishing lodging or food and drink; intrastate transportation of passengers
Nebraska	Telecommunications (including installation), telegraph, or community antenna television service; specific warranty and maintenance agreements
Nevada	Fabricating tangible personal property from materials provided by the customer
New Jersey	Processing and printing services; installation and maintenance; real estate maintenance and repair; storage and safe deposit rentals; advertising; telecommunications
New Mexico	Taxes generally all services
New York	Information services; processing and printing services; installation, repair, and maintenance of tangible personal property; real estate repair and

State	*Taxable Services*
	maintenance; motor vehicle parking and garaging; interior decorating and designing services; protective and detective services; telephone and telegraphy services; entertainment and information services
North Carolina	Does not generally tax services
North Dakota	Leasing of tangible personal property; sale of steam and gas; telecommunications; vulcanizing, recapping, and retreading services; furnishing bingo cards; providing accommodations; admissions
Ohio	Furnishing transient lodging; installing or repairing tangible personal property; washing, cleaning, or painting motor vehicles; industrial laundry services; data processing or computer services; telecommunications; landscaping and lawn care; private investigation and security services; building maintenance and janitorial services; employment services; exterminating services; physical fitness and recreation services; printing and photographic services; certain production and fabricating services
Oklahoma	Providing natural or artificial gas, electricity, ice, or steam; transportation for hire; telecommunications services; printing services; lodging services; parking or storage services; certain computer services; providing food or drink; advertising; use of health clubs; amusement admissions; vending machine sales; leases of tangible personal property; motion picture licensing; sales of floral items
Pennsylvania	Washing motor vehicles; installing or repairing tangible personal property; imprinting or printing services; laundry and dry cleaning; lobbying; credit and collection services; secretarial or editing services; disinfecting and pest control services; employment services; computer programming, data preparation, or storage; lawn care; self-storage

State	*Taxable Services*
Rhode Island	Processing or printing tangible personal property for consumers who furnish the materials used; furnishing or distributing tangible personal property by athletic or social clubs; furnishing meals or drinks
South Carolina	Does not tax services
South Dakota	Taxes generally all services
Tennessee	Renting tangible personal property; admissions; cable and satellite television services
Texas	Amusements; cable television; motor vehicle parking and services; repair and maintenance of tangible personal property; telecommunications; credit-reporting services; debt collection services; insurance services; information services; landscaping, lawn, and garbage services; data processing services; real property repair and maintenance services; private security services; and telephone-answering services
Utah	Transportation services; telephone and telegraph; utilities; furnishing meals; admissions; coin-operated car washes; repairs and maintenance of tangible personal property; cleaning of tangible personal property; providing transient lodging; laundry and dry cleaning; cable and satellite television (effective 7/1/03)
Vermont	Production, printing, or fabrication services
Virginia	Services included in or in connection with the sale of tangible personal property; fabrication of tangible personal property for customers who provided the materials; providing meals or drinks; transient lodging
Washington	Installation, repair, and alteration of tangible personal property; motor vehicle transportation, parking, and storage; transient lodging; amusement admissions; abstract, title, and escrow services; credit bureau services; landscape maintenance; renting or leasing tangible personal property; miscellaneous personal services
West Virginia	Taxes generally all services

State	*Taxable Services*
Wisconsin	Transient housing; admissions; telecommunications and cable television services; laundry services; photographic services; parking services; repair, cleaning, or towing services on tangible personal property; fabricating or printing services; landscaping or lawn services
Wyoming	Intrastate telephone service; intrastate transportation of passengers; utility services; meals and drinks, including cover charges; admissions; charges for repair or improvement of tangible personal property; contract scientific surveying

Planning Point 6-49. Taxpayers should be particularly careful about the treatment of services rendered in connection with tangible personal property. Many states do not tax the value of the services if they are separately stated from the price of the materials or the property installed, applied, or repaired. Similar treatment is given to separately stated freight charges.

Chapter 7

Amount of Tax

Although the sales price is the basis for determining the amount of sales and use tax, the states vary significantly in the elements that compose the selling price of an item. This chapter discusses the various components of the selling price.

Elements of Basis

Q 7:5 Are transportation and shipping charges included in the sales and use tax base?

The answer to this question varies depending upon when title passes and if the shipping charges are separately stated. If transportation and shipping are necessary to consummate the sale, they are usually deemed to be part of the purchase price and subject to tax. However, if title to the goods passes before delivery, then transportation and shipping might not be taxable if separately stated. (Sometimes separate statement alone is sufficient.) Generally, shipping charges are not taxable if separately stated in Arizona, Idaho, Illinois (and separately contracted), Indiana, Iowa, Kentucky, Maryland, New Jersey, Oklahoma, Virginia, and the District of Columbia. States requiring separate statement and shipment by common carrier include Alabama, Arkansas, California, Maine, Vermont, and West

Virginia. States requiring separate statement and FOB shipping point include Colorado, Florida, Georgia, Louisiana, Massachusetts, Nevada, North Dakota, South Carolina, Tennessee, Utah, and Washington. Shipping and transportation charges imposed after the sale has taken place are often deemed a tax-exempt service. In any case, vendors should separately state shipping charges as a protective and potential tax-savings measure.

Some states look to the Free on Board (FOB) point as determining where the sale takes place and the tax incurred. If a sale is quoted FOB shipping point, it indicates that the buyer is responsible for the transportation charges (even if prepaid by the seller), the sale occurs at the seller's dock, and, if separately stated, the shipping charges may be excluded from the sales tax base. [Whitehall Sand & Gravel Co. v. Tax Comm'n, 150 P.2d 370 (Utah 1944)] If a sale is quoted FOB destination, it is understood that the price quoted includes the shipping costs. The shipping costs are treated as an addition to the sales price. [Ames City v. Tax Comm'r, 71 N.W.2d 15 (Iowa 1955)] In some states, if the sales contract specifically states that the freight charges will be collected from the buyer, the vendor may be permitted to reduce the sales tax base by the amount of the charges. This may be the case even where only one price is quoted so long as the delivered price exceeds the shipping point price and the charges are separately stated.

Many states' regulations specifically address whether and when sales tax applies to transportation costs. Where the regulations are silent or ambiguous, the vendor can best avoid sales tax on transportation charges by complying with the following guidelines:

- Make the buyer assume responsibility for the freight charges.
- Charges for transportation should be billed separately following the sale.
- Shipping should be FOB shipping point via the mail or common carrier.
- Title should pass prior to shipping.
- Seller-paid transportation charges should be billed separately.

Although many purchasers may welcome the opportunity to reduce their sales tax costs, they may hesitate to accept the risk of loss associated with such practices.

Q 7:6 How do discounts, rebates, and other price reductions affect the determination of the sales and use tax base?

Whether a discount or rebate will reduce the sale price subject to tax can depend upon when the discount or rebate is made and by whom. Almost every state will reduce the sales tax base if a cash, trade, or volume discount is given at the time of sale. Discounts subject to a subsequent event such as prompt payment within 10 days, however, generally do not qualify as a reduction in the sales price. [*See, e.g.*, Kitsap-Mason Dairyman's Ass'n v. Washington, 467 P.2d 312 (Wash. 1970) and, more recently, Holyoke Gas and Electric Dept. v. Comm'r of Rev., and Town of Maysfield Municipal Lighting Dept. v. Comm'r of Rev., Nos. F224466 and F224467 (Mass. App. Tax Bd., May 9, 2002).]

Many states distinguish between "store" and "manufacturer's" coupons or rebates. "Store" coupons are issued directly by the retailer to the customer. Because the retailer is not reimbursed, the coupon represents a clear reduction in the sales price. "Manufacturer's" coupons are issued by the manufacturer, distributor, or wholesaler to the customer. Because the retailer is reimbursed, some states maintain there is no reduction in the sales prices and accordingly no reduction in the sales tax due. [*See, e.g.*, Keystone Chevrolet Co. v. Kirk, 372 N.E.2d 651 (Ill. 1978); Colorado, Special Regulations for Specific Businesses, Colorado's For Your Information (FYI Program) Coupons, Sales 22 (July 1993)]

The only states that allow a reduction in the taxable sales price for a manufacturer's coupon are Connecticut, Indiana, Kansas, and Texas. A manufacturer's rebate, rather than a coupon, is only allowed to reduce the sales price in Arizona (only if the retailer receives the reimbursement), Idaho (only applies to motor vehicle sales), Indiana, Louisiana (only applies to motor vehicle sales), Missouri, Utah, West Virginia, and Wyoming.

The only states that prohibit a reduction in the taxable sales price for cash discounts are Indiana, New Mexico, Ohio, Pennsylvania, and Vermont. The only states that prohibit a reduction in the taxable sales price for a retailer's own coupons are Indiana, New Mexico, and Pennsylvania.

Taxes

Q 7:12 Are taxes included in the sales price subject to sales and use taxes?

Certain federal excise taxes are included in the sales price for sales and use tax purposes. However, the states vary as to the ones they include or exclude. The following chart indicates whether a state includes or excludes a particular tax in the sales tax base.

Taxes Included in Sales and Use Tax Base

State	*Alcoholic Beverage Tax*	*Federal Gas Tax*	*Federal Luxury Excise Tax*	*Tobacco Tax*
Alabama	Yes			Yes, exempt if separately stated
Arizona	Yes			Yes
Arkansas	Yes	Yes		Yes
California	Yes			Yes
Colorado	Yes			Yes
Connecticut	Yes			Yes
District of Columbia	Yes			Yes
Florida	Yes			
Georgia	Yes	Yes		Yes
Hawaii	Yes		Yes	
Idaho	Yes			Yes
Illinois	Yes			Yes
Indiana	Yes			Yes
Iowa	Yes			Yes
Kansas		Yes	Yes	Yes
Kentucky	Yes			Yes
Louisiana	Yes	Yes	Yes	Yes
Maine	Yes		Yes	Yes
Maryland	Yes			Yes
Massachusetts	Yes	Yes	Yes	Yes
Michigan	Yes	Yes	Yes, unless separately stated	Yes
Minnesota	Yes			Yes
Mississippi	Yes			Yes
Missouri	Yes			
Nebraska	Yes			Yes
Nevada	Yes			Yes
New Jersey	Yes	Yes	No	Yes

State	Alcoholic Beverage Tax	Federal Gas Tax	Federal Luxury Excise Tax	Tobacco Tax
New Mexico			Yes	Yes
New York	Yes	Yes		Yes
North Carolina	Yes	Yes		Yes
North Dakota	Yes			Yes
Ohio	Yes		Yes	Yes
Oklahoma	Yes			Yes
Pennsylvania	Yes			Yes
Rhode Island	Yes			Yes
South Carolina	Yes			Yes
South Dakota	Yes		Yes	Yes
Tennessee	Yes			Yes
Texas			Yes	Yes
Utah	Yes			Yes
Vermont	Yes			Yes
Virginia	Yes		Yes	
Washington	Yes		Yes	Yes
West Virginia	Yes			
Wisconsin	Yes			
Wyoming	Yes			Yes

Gratuities and Tips

Q 7:15 Are gratuities or tips considered part of the sales tax base?

Voluntary gratuities or tips are generally not subject to sales tax, because they are excluded from the definition of "sales price." To qualify for exclusion, the tips must not only be voluntary but usually must also be separately stated and go to the servers or wait staff rather than the employer. Mandatory tips, for example, "a 15% gratuity will be added to groups of eight or more," are often deemed to be part of the sales price, because they are involuntary. That is, the sales prices for a meal with eight or more people will include an additional 15 percent charge. However, one court has ruled that even if involuntary, a mandatory tip going to the employees will not be taxable, because the employer receives no benefit from the gratuity. [Green v. Surf Club, Inc., 136 So. 2d 354 (Fla. Dist. Ct. App. 1961), *cert. denied,* 139 So. 2d 694 (Fla. 1962)] Some states also differentiate tips based upon the type of business. Banquet tips or tips for caterers may be treated differently than restaurant tips. Fortunately, most states have responded to this variation by issuing specific regulations or rulings distinguishing taxable from nontaxable tips. The following chart lists the states' treatment of mandatory tips.

Sales Tax Treatment of Mandatory Gratuities

Treatment	*State*
Taxable	Alabama, California, Connecticut (unless employer receives no benefit), District of Columbia, Florida (if any amount is retained by the employer), Georgia, Hawaii, Idaho (if customer is not advised in writing that they can change the amount), Illinois (unless the customer can change amount), Iowa, Kansas, Kentucky, Maine, Missouri (even if separately stated), Nebraska, Ohio, Rhode Island, South Carolina, South Dakota, Tennessee (unless customer can change the amount), Vermont, Virginia, Washington, West Virginia (unless customer can change amount), Wisconsin, and Wyoming.
Nontaxable	Arizona (if billed separately), Arkansas, Colorado, Indiana, Louisiana, Maryland, Massachusetts, Michigan (if separately stated), Minnesota (if separately stated), Mississippi (if separately stated), Nevada, New Jersey, New Mexico, New York (if all amounts are turned over to the employees), North Carolina (if not more than 15% and only those involved with providing the service share in the tip; the excess over 15% is subject to the sales tax; the entire amount is subject to the sales tax if others than those involved with providing the service share in the tip), North Dakota (if all amounts are given to the employees), Oklahoma (unless not paid to the employees or are used as part of the minimum wage), Pennsylvania (if separately stated), Texas, and Utah (unless management requires pooling or controls disbursement, then treated as a substitute for wages)

Chapter 8

Accounting Methods

Total taxable sales will vary with a business's accounting method. A cash basis taxpayer's monthly sales tax report may differ dramatically from the same sales reported on an accrual basis. As a consequence, most states have limited taxpayers' alternatives with respect to such accounting methodologies, including returns and allowances, bad debts, and installment sales.

Methods

Q 8:1 What accounting methods may be used in computing sales for sales tax purposes?

Taxpayers may elect to use the cash, accrual, or a hybrid of the two accounting methods in reporting their sales and use tax. The choice elected can seriously affect a company's cash flow. For example, a small business on an accrual basis may be forced to finance the sales tax on sales where the income has been earned but no cash has been collected.

States that generally require use of the accrual method of accounting include California, Florida, Idaho, Louisiana (except for rental payments and health club receipts), Maryland, Massachusetts, Michigan, Nevada, New Jersey, New York, North Dakota, Oklahoma, Pennsylvania, Rhode Island, South Carolina (but may use the cash method with written authorization), Tennessee, Utah, Vermont (but may use the cash method with written authorization), Virginia, and Wisconsin (but may use the cash method with written authorization).

In the following states a taxpayer may elect to report their sales tax on either a cash or accrual basis: Alabama, Arizona, Arkansas (cash may be used with permission), Colorado, Connecticut, Georgia, Hawaii, Illinois, Iowa, Kentucky (cash may be used with permission), Maine (cash may be used with permission), Minnesota, Mississippi (cash may be used with permission), Missouri, Nebraska, New Mexico, North Carolina, Ohio, South Carolina, South Dakota, Texas, Washington, West Virginia, Wisconsin (cash may be used with permission), Wyoming, and the District of Columbia.

Taxpayers must use the same accounting method for the state as they use for federal tax purposes in Hawaii, Indiana, Kansas, Maine, Nebraska, and West Virginia. Treasury regulations require that, where inventory is a significant income-producing factor, a business must use the accrual method of accounting for federal income tax purposes. [Reg. § 1.446-1(c)(2)(i)] Thus, the states that require sales tax to be reported on the same accounting basis as used for federal purposes are effectively requiring the use of accrual accounting.

Planning Point 8-1. Taxpayers using the accrual method of accounting may occasionally encounter customers that are unwilling to pay the tax. For significantly large dollar transactions, it is beneficial to have a procedure in place to verify that the customer agrees that they are taxable on the purchase, prior to remitting the tax to the state. Although there is very little time to do this, and still file the return on a timely basis, the extra effort in verifying the customer's tax status prior to remitting the tax to the state may avoid a costly and lengthy refund process with the state.

Returns of Taxable Property

Q 8:7 How do states handle the return of taxable property for sales tax purposes?

If a customer returns goods for a refund, most states allow the seller to deduct that sale from the taxable sales reported in the current period return. Other states allow the vendor to take a credit for the refunded sales tax rather than reduce taxable sales. Whether subtracted from gross sales or credited against tax due, either amount will be reduced by any customer restocking charge or handling fees, because they effectively reduce the amount that is returned to the customer. The following table lists the states' sales tax treatment of return goods.

State Sales Tax Treatment of Returned Goods

State Sales Treatment of Returned Goods	*States*
Credit for Returned Tax	Georgia (if more than 90 days after sale), Maryland (if tax was not remitted yet claims as a deduction), New York (credit or refund), North Carolina (credit or refund), North Dakota, Texas, Utah, Wyoming
Deducted from Gross Proceeds/Gross Sale	Alabama, Arkansas (if fully refunded), California (if fully refunded), Colorado (if fully refunded), Connecticut (if refund within 90 days of sales), Florida (refund or deduction), Georgia (if refund within 90 days of sales), Hawaii, Idaho, Illinois, Iowa, Kansas, Kentucky, Louisiana (unless tax was already remitted, then claim a refund), Maine (refund or deduction), Maryland (if tax was remitted, claim as credit), Massachusetts (for amounts returned to customer within 90 days of sale), Michigan, Minnesota, Mississippi, Missouri, Nebraska, Nevada, New Jersey (for amounts returned in the same or subsequent quarter), New Mexico, Ohio, Oklahoma, Pennsylvania,

State Sales Treatment of Returned Goods	*States*
	Rhode Island (if refunded within 120 days of sale), South Carolina, South Dakota, Tennessee, Vermont, Virginia, Washington, West Virginia, Wisconsin
Refund	District of Columbia, Florida (refund or deduction), Louisiana (if tax was remitted; if tax was not remitted yet, then a deduction from gross sales), New York (credit or refund), North Carolina (credit or refund)

Planning Point 8-2. Taxpayers claiming credit on previously taxed purchases should maintain careful notes regarding the month and return on which the tax was originally reported. In some instances, it may be advisable to maintain a separate file of refunds and returns that includes such information unless the volume of transactions would make it prohibitively expensive. In an audit, it is not unusual for the auditor to verify that tax was paid on any credits taken during the audit. Having easily accessible information will facilitate the review process and demonstrate diligence by the vendor.

Defaults on Sales

Q 8:8 How do states treat defaults on sales for sales tax purposes?

If a purchaser stops making payments, the vendor may repossess the property and resell it. Whether the sales tax can be recovered on the uncollected payments depends upon the vendor's method of accounting, the amount remitted to the state, any vendor's fee taken, and the amount refunded, if any, on the uncollected payments. In any case, the seller cannot recover more than the difference between what was remitted to the state and the amount collected from the customer. The following table lists the states' treatment of repossessions.

State Sales Tax Treatment of Repossessed Goods

State Treatment of Repossessed Goods	*States*
Deduction for Tax Refunded	Arkansas (if tax was fully refunded) California (if tax was fully refunded), Colorado (if tax was fully refunded), Florida (if tax was fully refunded), Georgia (deduction within 90 days; credit if after 90 days), Hawaii (if tax was fully refunded), Kansas (on unpaid portion of tax paid to state), Kentucky (on unpaid portion of tax paid to state), Maine, Massachusetts (if tax was fully refunded within 90 days), Nevada, New Mexico, New York, North Carolina, Ohio, Virginia, Washington, West Virginia, Wisconsin (if refund or net loss)
Credit	Alabama (for prepaid tax), Illinois (on uncollected portion of tax), Iowa (on bad-debt portion), Maryland (on uncollected portion of tax), Nebraska (on bad-debt portion), North Dakota (on uncollected portion of tax paid to state), Oklahoma (on uncollected portion of tax paid to state), South Dakota (on uncollected portion), Tennessee (on amounts in excess of $500), Texas, Utah, Vermont
No Refund or Credit	Arizona, Connecticut, District of Columbia, Idaho, Indiana, Louisiana (if property is saleable), Michigan, Minnesota, Mississippi, Missouri, New Jersey, Pennsylvania, Rhode Island, South Carolina, Wyoming

Chapter 9

Rates of Tax

Forty-five states and the District of Columbia impose a sales tax on retail sales of tangible personal property and selected services and a compensating use tax on the use or consumption of tangible personal property and selected services. This chapter discusses the tax rates used by state and local governments.

State Rate of Tax

Q 9:3 What is the range of general sales and use tax rates imposed by different states?

Not surprisingly, the range of sales and use tax rates varies from state to state. The state rates range from 2.9 percent to 7.00 percent. Local rates vary as well and are added to the state rate. For example, the combined state and local sales tax rate in New York City is 8.625 percent and 8.6 percent in Aspen, Colorado. Mississippi, Rhode Island, and Tennessee charge the highest state rate at 7.00 percent; Colorado is the lowest state tax rate at 2.9 percent. The following table lists the number of states using various tax rates.

State Sales Tax Rates

Statutory Tax Rates	*Number of States Imposing the Tax Rate*
7%	3
6.5%	3
6.25%	2
6%	9
5.75%	1 (District of Columbia)
5.6%	1
5.5%	1
5.3%	1
5.125%	1
5%	11
4.75%	1
4.5%	2
4.225%	1
4%	7
3.5%	1
2.9%	1

Q 9:4 What are the different sales and use tax rates used by each state?

The following table lists the general sales and use tax rates applied by the states and the District of Columbia. [*See* Q 9:6 for local sales and use tax rates.]

State Sales and Use Tax Rates (Noninclusive)

State	*Categories and State Sales and Use Tax Rates*
Alabama	Name: Sales and Use Taxes Local sales and use taxes are authorized. 4% of gross proceeds of sale or sales price 2% of sales of automotive vehicles or truck trailers, semi-trailers, house trailers, mobile homes, or travel trailers 1.5% on sales of machinery and equipment used in manufacturing, mining, processing, and farming 3% on sales of food sold through coin-operated vending machines

State	*Categories and State Sales and Use Tax Rates*
	5% of gross receipts on construction work involving any public highway, road, bridge, or street Name: Leasing or Rental Tax 4% of gross proceeds; reduced rate of 1.5% on the lease or rental of automotive vehicles or truck trailers, semi-trailers, or house trailers 2% on the lease or rental of linens and clothing
Alaska	No state sales and use tax, although cities and boroughs levy such taxes
Arizona	Name: Transaction Privilege and Use Taxes Local sales and use taxes are authorized. [See Chapter 20 for details.] 5.6% of gross proceeds of sales or gross income from the following business categories: amusements, contractors, personal property rental, pipelines, printers, private car lines, publishers, restaurants, retailers, telecommunications, transportation, and utilities 5.5% on transient lodgings 3.125% on mining
Arkansas	Name: Gross Receipts and Compensating Use Tax Local sales and use taxes are authorized. 5.125% on gross receipts of retail sales of tangible personal property and the following services: amusements, cable television, cleaning, lodging, photography, printing, telecommunications, and utilities 1% on short-term rentals of tangible personal property
California	Name: Sales and Use Taxes Local sales and use taxes are authorized. 6.00% of gross receipts or retail sales of tangible personal property
Colorado	Name: Sales and Use Taxes Local sales and use taxes are authorized. 2.9% of purchase price of exchanges and retail sales of tangible personal property and select

State	*Categories and State Sales and Use Tax Rates*
	services, including telecommunications, lodging, and utilities
Connecticut	Name: Sales and Use Taxes 6% of gross receipts or sales of tangible personal property and enumerated services (more than 150 different services are taxed) 12% of total rent received for transient lodging 2% on computer services
Delaware	Name: Manufacturers' License Requirements and Taxes $75 plus 0.18% of gross receipts exceeding $1 million per month Name: Retail and Wholesale Merchants' License Requirements and Taxes Wholesalers: $75 license fee per place of business plus 0.384% of gross receipts exceeding $50,000 per month. Food processors: $75 license fee per place of business plus 0.192% of gross receipts exceeding $50,000 per month Farm machinery dealer: $75 license fee per place of business plus 0.096% of aggregate gross receipts exceeding $50,000 per month Retailers: $75 license fee plus $25 per separate branch or business location plus 0.72% of gross receipts exceeding $50,000 per month Transient retailers: $25 license fee plus 0.72% of aggregate gross receipts from goods sold or services rendered in Delaware exceeding $3,000 per month Restaurant retailers: $75 license fee plus $25 per separate branch or business location plus 0.624% of aggregate gross receipts attributable exceeding $50,000 per month Contractors: $75 license fee per place of business plus 0.624% of aggregate gross receipts exceeding $50,000 per month Supermarket retailers: $75 license fee plus $25 per separate branch or business location plus

State	*Categories and State Sales and Use Tax Rates*
	0.384% applicable to the first $2 million of monthly gross receipts exceeding $50,000 and 0.72% applicable to all receipts over the first $2 million General Services: $75 license fee and an additional $25 per location plus .384% of gross receipts exceeding $50,000 per month
	Use tax on leases of tangible personal property: 1.92% of total rent plus license fee of 0.288% of rental payments exceeding $150,000 per quarter
District of Columbia	Name: Gross Sales and Compensating Sales Taxes
	5.75% on retail sales of tangible
	personal property and enumerated services, including rentals and admissions
	12% of gross receipts from motor vehicle parking or storage
	14.55% of gross receipts from transient lodging
	10% of gross receipts from sales of food or drink for immediate consumption
	8% of gross receipts from sales of spirituous or malt liquors, beer, and wine for off-premises consumption
Florida	Name: Tax on Sales, Use, and Other Transactions
	Local sales and use taxes are authorized.
	6% on retail sales of tangible personal property and enumerated services including
	Rentals and admissions
	9.17% on telecommunications services
	2.5% of sales price of self-propelled or power-drawn farm equipment
	4% on coin-operated amusement machine sales
Georgia	Name: Sales and Use Taxes
	Local sales and use taxes are authorized.
	4% on retail sales of tangible personal property and enumerated services, including rentals
Hawaii	Name: General Excise and Use Taxes

State	*Categories and State Sales and Use Tax Rates*
	4% on retail sales of tangible personal property and most services (Hawaii taxes more than 150 different services) 0.5% of gross sales of manufacturers, wholesalers, and agricultural producers
Idaho	Name: Sales and Use Taxes Local sales and use taxes are authorized. 5% on retail sales of tangible personal property and enumerated services
Illinois	Name: Retailer Occupation Tax Local sales and use taxes are authorized. 6.25% on retail sales of tangible personal property and enumerated services 1% reduced rate on retail sales of qualifying food, drugs, and medical appliances Name: Service Occupation and Service Use Taxes 6.25% of selling price of personalty transferred incident to a sale of service
Indiana	Name: Gross Retail and Use Tax 6% of gross sales
Iowa	Name: Sales and Use Taxes Local sales and use taxes are authorized. 5% on retail sales of tangible personal property and enumerated services, including rentals and admissions (Iowa taxes more than 70 different services)
Kansas	Name: Retailers' Sales and Compensating (Use) Tax Local sales and use taxes are authorized. 5.3% on retail sales of tangible personal property and enumerated services, including rentals and admissions; rental of motor vehicles is subject to an additional 3.5% excise tax
Kentucky	Name: Sales and Use Taxes 6% on retail sales of tangible personal property and enumerated services, including rentals and admissions

State	*Categories and State Sales and Use Tax Rates*
Louisiana	Name: Sales and Use Taxes Local sales and use taxes are authorized. 4% on retail sales of tangible personal property and enumerated services, including rentals and admissions
Maine	Name: Sales and Use Taxes 5% on retail sales of tangible personal property and enumerated services, including rentals and admissions 7% on the rental of transient lodgings and on liquor sold in licensed establishments 10% on the short-term (less than one year) rental of automobiles
Maryland	Name: Sales and Use Taxes 5% on retail sales of tangible personal property and enumerated services, including rentals and admissions
Massachusetts	Name: Sales and Use Taxes 5% on retail sales of tangible personal property and enumerated services
Michigan	Name: General Sales Tax Act, Use Tax Act 6% on retail sales of tangible personal property and enumerated services 4% reduced rate on residential use of utility services
Minnesota	Name: General Sales Tax Local sales and use taxes are authorized. 6.5% on retail sales of tangible personal property and enumerated services (Minnesota taxes more than 50 different services) 9% rate on sales of intoxicating liquor and 3.2 malt liquor 6.2% (plus an additional 3% depending on the lessor's volume) on the short-term (28 days or less) lease or rental of motor vehicles
Mississippi	Name: Sales and Use or Compensating Taxes 7% on retail sales of tangible personal property and enumerated services 3% on retail sales of aircraft, motor vehicles, and self-propelled equipment used in logging 1% on farm tractors

State	*Categories and State Sales and Use Tax Rates*
Mississippi	Name: Sales and Use Taxes Local sales and use taxes are authorized. 4.225% on retail sales of tangible personal property and enumerated services 4% reduced rate on motor vehicles, trailers, boats, and outboard motors
Nebraska	Name: Sales and Use Taxes Local sales and use taxes are authorized. 5.5% on retail sales of tangible personal property and enumerated services
Nevada	Name: Sales and Use Taxes Local sales and use taxes are authorized. 6.5% on retail sales of tangible personal property and enumerated services (2% rate plus 4.5% rate)
New Jersey	Name: Sales and Use Taxes 6% on retail sales of tangible personal property and enumerated services, including rentals and admissions
New Mexico	Name: Gross Receipts and Compensating Tax Local sales and use taxes are authorized. 5% on gross sales of tangible personal property and services (New Mexico taxes more than 115 different services)
New York	Name: Sales and Compensating Use Taxes Local sales and use taxes are authorized. 4% on retail sales of tangible personal property and enumerated services 5% additional tax on entertainment and information services
North Carolina	Name: Sales and Use Taxes Local sales and use taxes are authorized. 4.5% on retail sales of tangible personal property and enumerated services, including rentals and admissions 3% on aircraft, boats, and motor vehicles 6% on telecommunications 1% on farm machinery

State	*Categories and State Sales and Use Tax Rates*
North Dakota	Name: Sales and Use Taxes Local sales and use taxes are authorized. 5% on retail sales of tangible personal property and enumerated services, including rentals and admissions
Ohio	Name: Sales, Use, and Storage Taxes Local sales and use taxes are authorized. [See Chapter 21 for details.] 5% on retail sales of tangible personal property and enumerated services, including rentals and admissions (Ohio taxes more than 50 different services)
Oklahoma	Name: Sales and Use Taxes Local sales and use taxes are authorized. 4.5% on retail sales of tangible personal property and enumerated services, including rentals and admissions
Pennsylvania	Name: Sales and Use Taxes Local sales and use taxes are authorized. 6% on retail sales of tangible personal property and enumerated services, including rentals and admissions
Rhode Island	Name: Sales and Use Taxes 7% on retail sales of tangible personal property and enumerated services, including rentals and admissions Additional 5% tax on lodging
South Carolina	Name: Sales and Use Taxes Local sales and use taxes are authorized. 5% (4% for people age 85 and over) on retail sales of tangible personal property and enumerated services
South Dakota	Name: Retail Sales, Service, and Use Taxes Local sales and use taxes are authorized. 4% on retail sales of tangible personal property and services, including rentals and admissions (South Dakota taxes more than 140 different services)

State	*Categories and State Sales and Use Tax Rates*
	1% additional tax on lodging (camping, hotels, motels, etc.), car rentals, and amusements 3% reduced rate on agricultural equipment and oil and gas field services
Tennessee	Name: Sales and Use Taxes Local sales and use taxes are authorized. 7% on retail sales of tangible personal property and enumerated services, including rentals and admissions (Tennessee taxes more than 50 different services)
Texas	Name: Sales, Excise, and Use Taxes Local sales and use taxes are authorized. 6.25% on retail sales of tangible personal property and enumerated services, including rentals and admissions
Utah	Name: Sales and Use Taxes Local sales and use taxes are authorized. 4.75% on retail sales of tangible personal property and enumerated services, including rentals and admissions 2% on residential utility use
Vermont	Name: Sales and Use Taxes 5% on retail sales of tangible personal property and enumerated services, including rentals and admissions 4.36% on retail sales of Vermont telecommunication services
Virginia	Name: Retail Sales and Use Taxes Local sales and use taxes are authorized. 3.5% on retail sales of tangible personal property and enumerated services, including rentals and admissions 4% rate on vehicle rentals; 8% rate for daily vehicle rentals 3% rate on sale or use of motor vehicles 2% on air and watercraft
Washington	Name: Retail Sales and Use Taxes Local sales and use taxes are authorized.

State	*Categories and State Sales and Use Tax Rates*
	6.5% on retail sales of tangible personal property and enumerated services, including rentals and admissions
	5.9% additional rate added to retail car rentals
West Virginia	Name: Consumers; Sales and Use Taxes
	6% on retail sales of tangible personal property and enumerated services, including rentals and admissions
	3% on mobile homes used by the purchaser as permanent residence
Wisconsin	Name: General Sales and Use Taxes
	Local sales and use taxes are authorized.
	5% on retail sales of tangible personal property and enumerated services, including rentals and admissions
Wyoming	Name: Sales and Use Taxes
	Local sales and use taxes are authorized.
	4% on retail sales of tangible personal property and enumerated services, including rentals and admissions
	3% on farm equipment

Planning Point 9-3. Some states provide bracket or rate schedules of the sales tax to be collected on small taxable sales. In Nevada, for example, a retailer is required to use the state-provided bracket schedule unless an acceptable alternative is used. These bracket or rate schedules ease the collection process for smaller businesses. However, the vendor should be aware that the tax collected by use of such schedules might not be sufficient to pay the tax due on gross proceeds, receipts, or income (whichever term is used by the state).

Planning Point 9-4. Sales through vending machines are generally considered to have the tax included in the unit price of the merchandise. In those states in which sales tax is collected from the customer, the tax thus collected may be excluded from the total vending machine receipts to determine the base on which the tax liability is computed.

Example 9-1. ABC Vending has a vending machine located in a jurisdiction whose tax rate is 5 percent. The gross receipts from the machine this past month were $1,560. The taxable sales were $1,486 ($1,560 divided by 1.05), and the sales tax due is $74 ($1,486 times .05 or $1,560 minus $1,486).

Local Jurisdictions' Rate of Tax

Q 9:6 What are the rates used by local governments imposing a sales tax?

As with the states, the rates vary by local government, limited only by statutory (or sometimes constitutional) caps. The rates that may be applied are contained in the following table.

Local Governments' Sales Tax Rates

States	*Cities*	*Counties Boroughs*	*Special Districts*
Alabama	1.5–5%	1.5–5%	N/A
Arizona	0–6%	0–4.5%	N/A
Arkansas	.25–3%	.25–3%	N/A
California	1.25%	1.25%	.10–1.25%
Colorado	0–5.3%	0–5.3%	.1–6%
Florida	N/A	.5–1.5%	N/A
Georgia	N/A	1–4%	1%
Idaho	1–5%	1–5%	N/A
Illinois	0–1%	0–1%	0–.75%
Iowa	.5–2%	.5–2%	N/A
Kansas	.25–2%	.25–2%	N/A
Louisiana	0–5%	0–5%	N/A
Minnesota	.5–1%	.5–1%	N/A
Mississippi	.25–3%	.25–3%	0–3%
Missouri	1.25–2.5%	1.25–2.5%	0–1.5%
Nebraska	.5–1.5%	.5–1.5%	N/A
Nevada	N/A	4.5–5.25%	0–2%
New Mexico	.25–1.8125%	.25–1.8125%	N/A
New York	0–4.5%	0–4.5%	0–3%
North Carolina	N/A	2%	N/A
North Dakota	.5–2%	.5–2%	N/A

States	*Cities*	*Counties Boroughs*	*Special Districts*
Ohio	.25–3%	.25–3%	0–1.5%
Oklahoma	2–5%	2–5%	N/A
Pennsylvania	0–1%	0–1%	N/A
South Carolina	N/A	1–3%	0–3%
South Dakota	1–3%	N/A	N/A
Tennessee	2.75%	2.75%	N/A
Texas	.125–2%	.125–2%	0–1%
Utah	0–1%	0–1%	0–.5%
Virginia	1%	1%	N/A
Washington	.5–1.7%	.5–1.7%	0–.5%
Wisconsin	N/A	.1–.5%	0–3%
Wyoming	N/A	1–2%	N/A

Planning Point 9-5. In planning business expansion, location, and relocation, businesses frequently consider the rate of tax imposed by the state and local jurisdiction. For example, in many instances, by moving a business location across a border, substantial tax savings can be achieved. Care must be taken to consider both state and local tax rates. Colorado, for example, has a very low state sales tax rate of 2.9 percent, but its combined local sales and property taxes are among the highest in the country. While sales taxes are rarely a determinative factor in these types of decisions, they are frequently among the second tier of factors considered.

The impact of exemptions and exclusions from tax can also significantly affect such decisions. For example, a jurisdiction may impose a high rate of tax, but if it exempts manufacturing machinery and equipment, that may result in a substantial savings for the business and an inducement to locate or expand at that site. Taxpayers, therefore, need to consider the rates as well as the exemptions to properly evaluate the sales tax climate of a particular state and local jurisdiction.

Chapter 10

Returns or Reports

Unfortunately, the procedural and compliance burdens of sales and use tax can be as overwhelming as the interpretation of sales and use tax statutes. Errors in licensing, registration, filing deadlines, changes in ownership, and reporting procedures can often be as costly as errors in legal interpretation. This chapter addresses those issues.

Filing Requirements

Q 10:2 What forms must be submitted, and where are they sent?

The states provide the taxpayer with the necessary forms. The following chart lists the required tax forms and the mailing addresses where such forms should be sent.

Required Forms and Mailing Address

State	*Form*	*Mailing Address*
Alabama	Sales Tax: use Form 2100 Use Tax: use Form 2610	Alabama Department of Revenue Sales/Use Tax Division P.O. Box 327750 Montgomery, AL 36132-7750

State	Form	Mailing Address
Arizona	Sales and Use Taxes: use the same Form TPT-1	Department of Revenue P.O. Box 29010 Phoenix, AZ 85038-9010
Arkansas	Sales and Use Taxes: use the same Form ST-400	Department of Finance and Administration Sales and Use Tax Section P.O. Box 1272 Little Rock, AR 72203-1272
California	Sales and Use Taxes: use the same Form BT-401	State Board of Equalization P.O. Box 942879 Sacramento, CA 94279-0001
Colorado	Sales Tax: use Form DR-100 Use Tax: use Form DR-0252	Colorado Department of Revenue Attn: Sales and Use 1375 Sherman St. Denver, CO 80261
Connecticut	Sales and Use Taxes: use the same Form OS-114	Commissioner of Revenue Services 25 Sigourney St. Hartford, CT 06106
District of Columbia	Sales and Use Taxes: use the same Form FR-800M/ FR-800A	D.C. Government Post Office P.O. Box 679 Washington, DC 20044
Florida	Sales and Use Taxes: use the same Form DR-15	Florida Department of Revenue 5050 W. Tennessee St. Tallahassee, FL 32399-0100
Georgia	Sales and Use Taxes: use the same Form ST-3	Sales and Use Tax P.O. Box 105296 Atlanta, GA 30374-0390
Hawaii	Sales Tax: use Form G-45 Use Tax: use Form G-49	Various addresses
Idaho	Sales and Use Taxes: use the same Form 850	Idaho State Tax Commission P.O. Box 76 Boise, ID 83707-0076
Illinois	Sales and Use Taxes: use the same Form ST-1	Illinois Department of Revenue P.O. Box 19015 Springfield, IL 62794-9015
Indiana	Sales and Use Taxes: use the same Form ST-103	Indiana Government Center North P.O. Box 7218 Indianapolis, IN 46207-7218
Iowa	Sales Tax: use Form 31-004 Use Tax: use Form 232-001	Department of Revenue and Finance P.O. Box 10412 Des Moines, IA 50306-0412
Kansas	Sales Tax: use Form STD-16 Use Tax: use Form C-T9 Consumer Use Tax: use Form C-T10	Kansas Department of Revenue Business Tax Bureau P.O. Box 12001 Topeka, KS 66625-2001
Kentucky	Sales and Use Taxes: Use the same Form 51A-102 or 51A-103	Kentucky Revenue Cabinet 200 Fair Oaks Lane Frankfort, KY 40602-0003

State	Form	Mailing Address
Louisiana	Sales and Use Taxes: use the same Form R 1029	Department of Revenue and Taxation, Sales Tax Division P.O. Box 3138 Baton Rouge, LA 70821-3138
Maine	Sales and Use Taxes: use the same Form ST-7	Maine Revenue Services P.O. Box 1065 Augusta, ME 04332-1065
Maryland	Sales and Use Taxes: use the same Form ST-118	Tax Administration Remittance Processing Center 110 Carol St. Annapolis, MD 21411-0001
Massachusetts	Sales and Use Taxes: use the same Form ST-9	Department of Revenue 100 Cambridge St. P.O. Box 9689 Boston, MA 02114
Michigan	Sales and Use Taxes: use the same Form 160	Michigan Department of Treasury Sales and Use Tax Treasury Bldg. Lansing, MI 48922
Minnesota	Sales and Use Taxes: N/A	All returns must be filed either by phone or electronically. Payments may be sent to Minnesota Department of Revenue P.O. Box 64622 St. Paul, MN 55146-0622
Mississippi	Sales Tax: use Form 72-010 Use Tax: use Form 72-110	Mississippi State Tax Commission P.O. Box 960 Jackson, MS 39205
Missouri	Sales Tax Form: use Form DOR 53-1 Use Tax Form: use Form DOR 53-U	Department of Revenue Business Tax Bureau P.O. Box 840 Jefferson City, MO 65105-0840
Nebraska	Sales and Use Taxes: use the same Form 10	Nebraska Department of Revenue P.O. Box 98923 301 Centennial Mall South Lincoln, NE 68509-8923
Nevada	Sales and Use Taxes: use the same Form TXR-01.01 Consumer Use Tax: use Form TXR-01.02	State of Nevada Department of Taxation 1550 E. College Parkway, Suite 115 Carson City, NV 89706
New Jersey	Sales and Use Taxes: use the same Form ST-50 or ST-51	State of New Jersey Division of Taxation P.O. Box 240 Trenton, NJ 08695
New Mexico	Sales and Use Taxes: use the same Form CRS-1	New Mexico Revenue Department P.O. Box 630 Santa Fe, NM 87504

State	*Form*	*Mailing Address*
New York	Sales and Use Taxes: use the same form ST-100	Various addresses
North Carolina	Sales and Use Taxes: use the same Form E-500	North Carolina Department of Revenue P.O. Box 25000 Raleigh, NC 27640
North Dakota	Sales and Use Taxes: use the same Form S-1 or S-2	North Dakota Office of State Tax Commissioner Sales and Special Taxes Division State Capitol Bldg. 600 E. Boulevard Ave. Bismarck, ND 58505-0599
Ohio	Sales Tax: use Form ST-10, ST-100, or ST-10T Use Tax: use Form UT-1018, UT-1014, or UT-902A	Treasurer, State of Ohio P.O. Box 16560 Columbus, OH 43216-6560
Oklahoma	Sales Tax: use Form STS-001 or STS-002 Use Tax: use Form 21-1 or 21-3	Oklahoma Tax Commission Attn: Sales Tax Division 2501 Lincoln Blvd. Oklahoma City, OK 73194
Pennsylvania	Sales and Use Taxes: use the same Form PA-3	Pennsylvania Receipts & Control Harrisburg, PA 17128-0406
Rhode Island	Sales and Use Taxes: use the same Form T-204 or T-204R if file monthly; Form Q-204 if file quarterly	Rhode Island Division of Taxation One Capital Hill, Suite 4 Providence, RI 02908-5802
South Carolina	Sales and Use Taxes: use the same Form ST-3, ST-388, or ST-403	South Carolina Department of Revenue P.O. Box 125 Columbia, SC 29214
South Dakota	Sales and Use Taxes: use the same Form Sales & Use Tax Return	Remit Center P.O. Box 5055 Sioux Falls, SD 57117
Tennessee	Sales and Use Taxes: use the same Form 07-003-117	Department of Revenue Sales and Use Tax Division 500 Deadrick St. Andrew Jackson State Office Bldg. Nashville, TN 37242
Texas	Sales and Use Taxes: use the same Form 01-114	Comptroller of Public Accounts 111 E. 17th St. Austin, TX 78744-0100
Utah	Sales and Use Taxes: use the same Form TC-71	State Tax Commission 210 N. 1950 W Salt Lake City, UT 84134-0400

State	Form	Mailing Address
Vermont	Sales and Use Taxes: use the same Form SU-451	Vermont Department of Taxes 109 State St. P.O. Box 547 Montpelier, VT 05601-0547
Virginia	Sales and Use Taxes: use the same Form ST-9	Department of Taxation Processing Services Division P.O. Box 1103 Richmond, VA 23218-1103
Washington	Sales and Use Taxes: use the same Form Combined Excise Tax Return	Department of Revenue P.O. Box 34054 Seattle, WA 98124-1054
West Virginia	Sales Tax: use Form WV/CST-200 Use Tax: use Form WV/CST-220	West Virginia Tax Department P.O. Box 1826 Charleston, WV 25327-1826
Wisconsin	Sales and Use Taxes: use the same Form ST-12	Wisconsin Department of Revenue P.O. Box 93389 Milwaukee, WI 53293-0389
Wyoming	Sales and Use Taxes: use the same ETS Forms 10 or 11	Department of Revenue Herschler Bldg. 122 W. 25th St. Cheyenne, WY 82002-0110

Planning Point 10-3. Most states will accept photocopies of returns, so long as they are the same size, shape, and approximate thickness of the original. When submitting copies of a subsidiary company's return, all coded and preprinted references should be eliminated. Many returns are encoded like checks with information to identify the filing period and taxpayer. A failure to eliminate these references could result in confusion between related company filings.

Many taxpayers subscribe to services that provide return copies for a relatively nominal charge. Some programs even allow for electronic completion and submission of the data. In addition, most state Web sites provide downloadable forms that can be completed and submitted. In some states, the forms may even be filled out on-line. State and local tax services also offer form publications that can be purchased. These include copies of all commonly used forms.

Q 10:3 Will states accept reproductions of the sales and use tax return?

Most states accept reproduced sales and use tax forms. However, states that use computer-generated or optically scanned returns are more likely to disallow the use of copies. The states that do not allow the use of reproduced forms or copies are Alabama, Arizona, Florida, Idaho, Illinois (unless computer generated and with prior approval), Kentucky, Louisiana, Maine, Maryland, Michigan, Minnesota, Mississippi, North Carolina, Pennsylvania, South Carolina (unless prior approval), South Dakota, Tennessee, Vermont, West Virginia, Wisconsin, and Wyoming (unless preapproved).

Extension of Time

Q 10:10 Can a taxpayer get an extension of time to file a sales and use tax return?

Most of the states will grant extensions, but usually only upon written request and for "good cause." "Good cause" is a term of art and varies from state to state but usually includes business disruptions due to natural disasters including flood and fire, strikes by employees, death of key personnel, hospitalization, etc. Lack of funds does not constitute good cause in those states where the vendor is collecting the tax from the purchaser for remittance to the state. The District of Columbia and the following 13 states do not allow extensions: Arizona, Arkansas, Florida, Illinois, Indiana, Maryland, Michigan, Nebraska, New Jersey, Ohio, Pennsylvania, South Dakota, and Utah. Vermont has granted extensions, but rarely. For those states granting extensions, the period extended varies from 5 days to 12 months, as indicated in the following table.

Maximum Term of Filing Extension

State	*Period*
Alabama	30 days
Arizona	N/A
Arkansas	N/A
California	One month
Colorado	5 to 15 days
Connecticut	Department discretion
District of Columbia	30 days
Florida	N/A
Georgia	End of month
Hawaii	90 days

State	*Period*
Idaho	One month
Illinois	N/A
Indiana	N/A
Iowa	30 days
Kansas	60 days
Kentucky	30 days
Louisiana	30 days
Maine	30 days
Maryland	N/A
Massachusetts	6 months
Michigan	N/A
Minnesota	60 days
Mississippi	30 days
Missouri	60 days
Nebraska	N/A
Nevada	30 days
New Jersey	N/A
New Mexico	12 months
New York	3 months
North Carolina	30 days
North Dakota	30 days
Ohio	N/A
Oklahoma	15 days
Pennsylvania	N/A
Rhode Island	30 days
South Carolina	30 days
South Dakota	N/A
Tennessee	30 days
Texas	45 days
Utah	N/A
Vermont	Rarely given
Virginia	30 days
Washington	30 days
West Virginia	30 days
Wisconsin	30 days
Wyoming	90 days

Consolidated Returns

Q 10:11 May a consolidated sales and use tax return be filed if a taxpayer operates more than one site in a state?

Yes, although several states require a minimum number of locations before a taxpayer may file a consolidated return. Only North Dakota, South Carolina, and Tennessee prohibit consolidated sales and use tax returns.

Nineteen states and the District of Columbia require the taxpayer to get prior permission before filing a consolidated tax return. Those states are California, Connecticut, Florida (in the form of a consolidated registration number), Georgia, Illinois, Kansas, Kentucky, Louisiana, Maine, Maryland, Mississippi, Nebraska, New Jersey, Ohio, South Dakota, Vermont, Virginia, Washington, and Wisconsin (each location must be registered with only one permit number).

Q 10:12 If a business operates on a divisional basis, are the divisions allowed to file separate sales and use tax returns?

Corporate divisions may elect to file separate sales and use tax returns in Arizona, Arkansas, Colorado, Connecticut, Florida, Georgia, Illinois, Indiana, Kansas, Kentucky, Louisiana, Maine, Maryland, Michigan (if separately licensed), Minnesota, Mississippi, Missouri, Nebraska, Nevada, New Jersey, New Mexico, New York, North Carolina, North Dakota, Ohio, Pennsylvania, Rhode Island, South Carolina, South Dakota, Tennessee (if more than one location), Vermont (a separate account number is required for each location), Washington, West Virginia, Wyoming, and the District of Columbia.

Alabama, California, Hawaii, Idaho, Iowa, Massachusetts, Oklahoma, Texas, Utah, Virginia, and Wisconsin do not permit separate divisional sales and use tax returns.

Chapter 11

Payment

The actual payment procedures for sales and use tax collected or accrued by a taxpayer vary almost as much as the interpretation of the sales and use tax laws themselves. Variations among the states exist in the date payment is due, the need for bond or security requirements, the discounts available for prompt payment, and the requirements for payment by electronic fund transfer.

Discount for Prompt Payments

Q 11:4 Do states give prompt-payment discounts?

Prompt-payment discounts (also known as accounting, service, and vendor compensation fees) are offered by many states to encourage the prompt collection, reporting, and payment of sales and use taxes. The discounts or vendor's fees not only encourage retailer compliance but also mitigate the seller's cost of accounting for and remitting the taxes. The following chart summarizes the states' discount rate for vendors:

State Sales and Use Tax Discount Rates

State	*Discount Rate*
Alabama	5% on the first $100; 2% thereafter to a maximum of $400 per month; 3% for use tax
Arizona	1% of tax due; $10,000 maximum per calendar year
Arkansas	2% to a maximum of $1,000 per month
California	Not allowed
Colorado	2.33% of tax collected
Connecticut	Not allowed
District of Columbia	The lesser of 1% of tax remitted or $5,000
Florida	2.5% of the first $1,200 of tax remitted
Georgia	3% of the first $3,000 tax remitted; 0.5% of balance
Hawaii	Not allowed
Idaho	Not allowed
Illinois	1.75% of tax remitted
Indiana	1%
Iowa	Not allowed
Kansas	Not allowed
Kentucky	1.75% of the first $1,000; 1% on balance
Louisiana	1.1%
Maine	Not allowed
Maryland	.06% on first $6,000; .045% on balance
Massachusetts	Not allowed
Michigan	0.75% discount allowed for payments by the 7th of the month; 0.5% between the 7th and the 15th; but discount only applies to the first 4% of tax collected
Minnesota	Not allowed
Mississippi	2% with maximum of $50 per return and $600 per year
Missouri	2%
Nebraska	2.5% of the first $3,000 per month; 0.5% on balance
Nevada	1.25%
New Jersey	Not allowed
New Mexico	Not allowed

State	*Discount Rate*
New York	3.5% of tax remitted, with a maximum of $150 per quarter
North Carolina	Not allowed
North Dakota	1.5%, with a maximum of $85 per month
Ohio	.75%
Oklahoma	2.25%, with a maximum of $3,300 per month
Pennsylvania	1%
Rhode Island	Not allowed
South Carolina	2%, with a maximum of $3,000 annually; 3% for tax liabilities less than $100
South Dakota	Not allowed
Tennessee	Not allowed
Texas	0.5% except for direct-pay permit holders
Utah	1.5% of state tax and 1% of local, special district, and use taxes
Vermont	Not allowed
Virginia	Graduated: 4% up to $62,500; 3% from $62,501 to $208,000; 2% on amounts over $208,000
Washington	Not allowed
West Virginia	Not allowed
Wisconsin	Greater of 0.5% or $10, but not more than tax
Wyoming	Not allowed

Example 11-1. The calculation of a prompt-payment discount for sales tax depends on the state involved. If a vendor makes net taxable sales of $550,000 during the month, the prompt-payment discount would be calculated as follows:

If the vendor operates in Georgia:

Net Taxable Sales	$550,000.00
Multiplied by Sales Tax Rate	× .04
Sales Tax	$ 22,000.00
Discount:	
$3,000 × .03 =	$ 90.00
plus ($22,000 − $3,000) × .005 =	+ 95.00
	$ 185.00

If the vendor operates in Nebraska:

Net Taxable Sales	$550,000.00
Multiplied by Sales Tax Rate	× .05
Sales Tax	$ 27,500.00
Discount:	
$3,000 × .025 =	$ 75.00
plus ($27,500 − $3,000) × .005 =	122.50
	$ 197.50

Planning Point 11-4. In most states, the vendor discounts or other compensation is only allowed for amounts reported as sales tax. Because the underlying reason for these discounts is to compensate vendors for the additional effort and record keeping required for sales tax compliance, providing a discount on taxpayers' use tax obligation would provide a discount without the additional effort that is required for sales tax compliance.

Direct-Payment Permits

Q 11:5 Do the states recognize direct-payment permits for sales and use tax?

Yes. Several states provide direct-payment permits for taxpayers purchasing a significant amount of property and services. The direct-pay permit enables the taxpayer to make all of its purchases free from tax and then self-assess use tax on those transactions that are properly taxable. One advantage to the direct-pay permit is that larger taxpayers making purchases from thousands of vendors need not rely on those vendors to properly charge tax. Instead, the "to tax or not to tax" decision is made by the purchaser who best knows how the property is being used. Thirty-eight states issue direct-pay permits: Alabama, Arizona, Arkansas, California, Colorado, Connecticut, Georgia, Idaho, Illinois, Indiana, Iowa, Kansas, Kentucky, Louisiana, Maine, Maryland, Massachusetts, Michigan, Minnesota, Mississippi, Missouri, Nebraska, New Jersey, New York, North Carolina, North Dakota, Ohio, Oklahoma, Pennsylvania, South Carolina, South Dakota, Tennessee, Texas, Vermont, Virginia, West Virginia, Wisconsin, and Wyoming.

The following states and the District of Columbia do not issue direct-pay permits: Florida, Hawaii, Nevada, New Mexico, Rhode Island, Utah, and Washington.

Planning Point 11-5. The decision by a state to grant a taxpayer direct-pay status is generally dependent upon the following factors:

- Is the general operation of the taxpayer of the nature that would lead to substantial uncertainty of use at the time the item is purchased? Generally, the types of businesses that qualify for direct-pay status are construction contractors with varied operations, manufacturers, and other multistate operations.
- Does the taxpayer have adequate procedures in place to make the use tax determination at the time the item is placed into use, and is the taxpayer willing to be responsible for reporting such amounts?
- Many states require that the taxpayer show some benefit to the state in granting the direct-pay status. For example, allowing a taxpayer to have a direct-payment status may simplify the auditing process for a particular state.

Once a state grants a taxpayer direct-payment status, the state usually requires that the taxpayer agree to be audited every year and submit its data-gathering procedures for review. There may be higher penalties and interest rates for underpayment of use tax liability.

Electronic Funds Transfers

Q 11:6 Do states require taxpayers to use electronic funds transfers to pay their sales and use tax liabilities?

The majority of the states require the use of electronic funds transfers (EFT) once tax collection exceeds a set floor, which varies from state to state. EFT is a method of transferring funds automatically through an organization associated with the Federal Reserve called the Automated Clearing House (ACH). The ACH provides a nationwide electronic network that serves as an interbank clearinghouse for electronic payments for any participating financial institution.

States Requiring the Use of Electronic Funds Transfers for Sales and Use Taxes

State	*Conditions*
Alabama	If monthly tax liability is at least $25,000
Arizona	If prior year's tax liability was at least $1 million
Arkansas	If average monthly tax liability is $20,000
California	If average monthly liability is at least $20,000; those not required to use EFT may be allowed to use EFT
Colorado	If prior year's tax liability exceeded $75,000
Connecticut	If tax liability was more than $100,000 during the last 12 months
Florida	If prior year's tax liability was at least $50,000
Georgia	If payments are more than $10,000 per month
Hawaii	If annual tax liability is more than $100,000
Idaho	For payments of at least $100,000
Illinois	If tax liability for preceding calendar year was $200,000 or more
Indiana	If prior or current year's tax liability exceeds $10,000 per quarter
Iowa	If semi-monthly liability exceeds $4,000 and for all direct-pay permit taxpayers
Kansas	If total sales tax liability exceeds $100,000 in any calendar year
Kentucky	If monthly liability exceeds $10,000
Louisiana	If tax liability exceeds $20,000 per payment
Maine	If annual payments are $400,000 or more
Maryland	If payments with return exceed $20,000
Massachusetts	If annual liability is at least $250,000
Michigan	When tax liability in prior year was $720,000 or more; others may use EFT
Minnesota	If liability during prior fiscal year ending June 30 was at least $120,000
New Jersey	If prior year's tax liability was $20,000 or more
New Mexico	If prior year's monthly average liability was $25,000 or more
New York	If prior year's sales and use tax liability was more than $1 million (EFT or certified check)

State	*Conditions*
North Carolina	If monthly average required payment was at least $20,000
Ohio	If sales and use tax obligation was at least $60,000 in a calendar year
Oklahoma	If tax liability exceeds $25,000 per month (effective March 1, 2002)
Pennsylvania	If tax liability is $20,000 or more per filing period (EFT, certified check, or cashier's check is acceptable)
Rhode Island	If tax liability exceeds $10,000
Tennessee	If payments are expected to average $10,000 or more
Texas	If tax liability exceeds $100,000 per tax type during preceding fiscal year
Utah	If prior year's sales and use tax liability was $96,000 or more
Virginia	If average monthly sales and use tax liability exceeds $20,000
Washington	When annual tax liability exceeds $240,000
Wisconsin	If prior calendar year tax liability exceeded $10,000

States that do not require the use of EFTs include Mississippi, Missouri, Nebraska (may use EFTs voluntarily), Nevada, North Dakota, South Carolina, South Dakota, Vermont, West Virginia, and Wyoming; in addition, the District of Columbia does not require the use of EFTs.

Q 11:7 Does the state or the taxpayer initiate use of EFTs for payments of sales and use taxes?

EFT participation is not automatic. The state and taxpayer must both agree to use EFTs for transferring tax payments. The following chart indicates whether the state or the taxpayer initiates contact for EFT payments.

Initiation of EFTs

Who Initiates EFT Payments	*States*
Taxpayers contacted by state before beginning EFT	Arkansas, Connecticut, Georgia, Kansas, Kentucky, Missouri, New Jersey, New York, North Carolina, Ohio (if required), South Carolina, Texas, Utah, Washington, Wyoming
If not contacted by state, taxpayer needs state permission to begin EFT	Alabama, California, Colorado, District of Columbia, Florida, Hawaii, Idaho, Illinois, Indiana, Iowa, Louisiana, Maine, Massachusetts, Michigan, Nebraska, Oklahoma (voluntarily use EFT), Rhode Island, South Dakota, Tennessee
If not contacted by state, taxpayer does not need state permision to begin EFT	Arizona (taxpayer needs to complete authorization agreement), Maryland, Minnesota, New Mexico, Pennsylvania, Virginia

Q 11:8 Which type of EFT transaction is used by the states?

An EFT may be accomplished either as a credit or as a debit transaction. The difference between the two is simply who originates the transaction. Credit transactions are originated by the taxpayer and debit transactions by the state. The following table indicates the type of EFT method used by the states.

EFT Method Used by the States

Methods	*States*
Debit Only	Indiana, New Mexico, Virginia
Credit Only	Maine
Both Debit and Credit	Alabama, Arizona, Arkansas, California, Colorado, Connecticut, District of Columbia, Florida (credit method if requested and approved), Georgia,

Methods	*States*
	Hawaii, Idaho, Illinois (credit method with prior approval), Iowa, Kansas, Louisiana, Maryland, Massachusetts, Michigan, Minnesota, Nebraska, New Jersey, New York, North Carolina (credit method with prior approval), North Dakota, Ohio, Oklahoma, Pennsylvania, Rhode Island, South Carolina, South Dakota, Tennessee, Texas, Utah, Washington
Others	Arizona (debit/credit/wire transfer), California (debit/credit/wire transfer with prior permission in emergency situations), Colorado (credit card), Kentucky, New York (certified check), Ohio (debit/credit/wire transfer), Pennsylvania (debit/credit/cashier's check delivered by courier), South Carolina (debit/credit/wire transfer in emergency situations), Texas (debit/credit/wire transfer in emergency situations), Wyoming (debit/wire)

Chapter 12

Refunds and Credits

Every state with a sales tax also provides for either a refund or credit of the tax due for overpayments in the case of bad debts, repossessions, returned goods, or errors of misinterpretation or simple calculation. This chapter discusses the states' treatment of refunds and credits.

Refunds

Q 12:2 How does a taxpayer obtain a refund or credit of sales tax?

The steps for claiming a sales tax refund or credit vary by state, but the most common procedures include (1) adjusting the sales reported or tax due on a following return; (2) amending the original return; or (3) filing a separate refund claim either by letter or specific form. The following chart summarizes the alternatives that each state has indicated that it will accept (other options may be available):

	Adjust next Report	*Amend Original*	*File Refund Claim*
Alabama	X	X	X
Arizona		X	
Arkansas		X	

	Adjust next Report	*Amend Original*	*File Refund Claim*
California			
Colorado	X		X
Connecticut	X	X	X
District of Columbia			X
Florida	X		X
Georgia	X	X	X
Hawaii	X	X	
Idaho	X		X
Illinois			X
Indiana	X		X
Iowa	X		
Kansas		X	X
Kentucky	X		
Louisiana		X	X
Maine	X		
Maryland	X		X
Massachusetts		X	X
Michigan	X	X	
Minnesota	X	X	X
Mississippi	X	X	
Missouri		X	X
Nebraska	X		
Nevada	X	X	X
New Jersey		X	X
New Mexico	X	X	X
New York	X		X
North Carolina	X	X	X
Ohio	X	X	X
Oklahoma	X	X	
Pennsylvania			X
Rhode Island		X	X
South Carolina		X	X
South Dakota	X		
Tennessee	X		
Texas	X	X	
Utah	X	X	X
Vermont	X		
Virginia	X	X	

	Adjust next Report	Amend Original	File Refund Claim
Washington	X		
West Virginia		X	X
Wisconsin	X		
Wyoming		X	X

Planning Point 12-3. Traditionally purchasers were required to request refund claims through their vendors, who are then obligated to file the refund claims on behalf of their customers. This approach provided safeguards for the state by ensuring that there were no duplicate refunds. With the growth of reverse audits and sales and use tax recovery work, many vendors find that filing refund claims on behalf of their customers is a time-consuming and unproductive activity. Therefore, some states have adopted streamlined procedures that allow the vendor to assign the right to receive the refund to their customer. Once the assignment is executed, the customer can then deal directly with the state in obtaining a refund of sales taxes paid in error. Before filing a refund claim with a vendor, taxpayers should check with the state to determine if an assignment is feasible.

Planning Point 12-4. Although many states allow vendors to offset future sales tax with credits or adjustments from the current period, virtually no state allows the offset of sales tax against use tax due or vice versa. Care should be exercised to make sure these offsets are properly managed to avoid unnecessary liabilities in the future.

Q 12:7 What is the effect of a state's statute of limitations on sales and use tax refunds?

In tax law, the statute of limitations is a legal provision that limits the amount of time that the government can make a tax assessment or the taxpayer can make a refund claim. The statute of limitations is generally the same; however, it can vary with the type of tax involved (income, estate, property, or sales), the amount of understatement, and whether or not returns have been filed. Generally, if the taxpayer has committed fraud or never filed a return, there is no statute of limitations on tax assessments. However, there may be a limit to refund claims even where no return has been filed. The following table summarizes the states' statutes of limitations for sales and use tax.

General Statute of Limitations for Sales and Use Tax

Statute of Limitations	*States*
3 Years	Alabama, Arkansas, California, Colorado, Connecticut, District of Columbia, Florida, Georgia, Hawaii, Idaho, Indiana, Iowa, Kansas, Louisiana, Maine, Massachusetts, Mississippi, Missouri, Nebraska, Nevada, New Mexico, New York, North Carolina, Oklahoma, Pennsylvania, Rhode Island, South Carolina, South Dakota, Tennessee, Utah, Vermont, Virginia, West Virginia, Wyoming
3.5 Years	Illinois (3 to 3.5), Minnesota
4 Years	Arizona, Kentucky, Maryland, Michigan, New Jersey, Ohio, Texas, Wisconsin
5 Years	Washington
6 Years	North Dakota

Planning Point 12-7. Sales and use tax returns should be reviewed periodically to determine whether the returns were correctly prepared. The period for reviewing the returns should be short enough so that refund claims can be filed and any correspondence with the state can be completed before the statute of limitations expires.

Chapter 14

License and Registration

Licensing and registration are the entry points into each state's sales tax system. This chapter discusses the different procedures states use to register and track licensed vendors.

Communication with Registrants

Q 14:16 How do the states communicate with permit holders?

Traditionally, new registrants receive introductory booklets of various length and quality explaining the basics of sales and use tax, common taxable and exempt transactions, and filing instructions. Many state revenue departments offer free one- or two-hour classes for new licensees. Other states publish periodic bulletins or newsletters to cover new legislation, court decisions, and general educational material about the state's taxes. Sometimes the booklets, classes, and bulletins target specific business types or industries.

Planning Point 14-2. Many states have now developed sophisticated Web sites that include their press releases, newsletters, bulletins, tax statutes, etc. They may also include downloadable data, such as forms and instructions for taxpayers' use. For taxpayers with Internet access, this may be the least expensive way to obtain information about changes in the tax laws. Taxpayers should keep in mind, however, that the information provided will only reflect the state's position on any given issue.

Internet Addresses

State	*Internet address*
Alabama	http://www.ador.state.al.us/
Alaska	http://www.revenue.state.ak.us/
Arkansas	http://www.state.ar.us/dfa/
Arizona	http://www.revenue.state.az.us/
California (FTB)	http://www.ftb.ca.gov/
California (SBE)	http://www.boe.ca.gov/
Colorado	http://www.revenue.state.co.us/
Connecticut	http://www.drs.state.ct.us/
Delaware	http://www.state.de.us/revenue/
District of Columbia	http://cfo.dc.gov/etsc/services/business_tp.shtm
Florida	http://www.state.fl.us/dor/
Georgia	http://www.state.ga.us/departments/dor/
Hawaii	http://www.state.hi.us/tax/tax.html
Idaho	http://www.state.id.us/tax/
Illinois	http://www.revenue.state.il.us/
Indiana	http://www.in.gov/dor/
Iowa	http://www.state.ia.us/government/drf/
Kansas	http://www.ink.org/public/kdor
Kentucky	http://www.state.ky.us/agencies/revenue/revhome.htm
Louisiana	http://www.rev.state.la.us/
Maine	http://state.me.us/revenue/
Maryland	http://www.comp.state.md.us/
Massachusetts	http://www.dor.state.ma.us/
Michigan (Treasury)	http://www.treas.state.mi.us/
Minnesota	http://www.taxes.state.mn.us./
Mississippi	http://www.mstc.state.ms.us/
Missouri	http://dor.state.mo.us/
Montana	http://www.state.mt.us/revenue/
Nebraska	http://www.revenue.state.ne.us/
Nevada	http://www.tax.state.nv.us/
New Hampshire	http://webster.state.nh.us/revenue/
New Jersey	http://www.state.nj.us/treasury/taxation/
New Mexico	http://www.state.nm.us/tax/
New York	http://www.tax.state.ny.us/
North Carolina	http://www.dor.state.nc.us/
North Dakota	http://www.state.nd.us/taxdpt/

State	*Internet address*
Ohio	http://www.state.oh.us/tax/
Oklahoma	http://www.oktax.state.ok.us/
Oregon	http://www.dor.state.or.us/
Pennsylvania	http://www.revenue.state.pa.us/
Rhode Island	http://www.tax.state.ri.us/tax/
South Carolina	http://www.sctax.org
South Dakota	http://www.state.sd.us/drr2/revenue.html
Tennessee	http://www.state.tn.us/revenue/
Texas	http://www.window.state.tx.us/
Utah	http://tax.ex.state.ut.us/
Vermont	http://www.state.vt.us/tax/
Virginia	http://www.tax.state.va.us/
Washington	http://www.dor.wa.gov/
West Virginia	http://www.state.wv.us/taxdiv/
Wisconsin	http://www.dor.state.wi.us/
Wyoming	http://revenue.state.wy.us/

Chapter 15

Audits

The word audit comes down to us from the Latin word *auditus*, or the act of hearing. The term is particularly appropriate for in the ancient and medieval world when most people were illiterate, "hearing" is an apt description of a medieval auditor's responsibilities. Obviously, the tools of an auditor today have changed, as have the recordkeeping responsibilities of those being audited. Furthermore, auditing for sales and use tax, although based on the general principles and techniques of financial statement auditing, has its own particular goals, procedures, guidelines, and tools. In this chapter we address how sales and use tax audits are chosen, how they are conducted, the role of sampling, and how best to prepare for these examinations.

Administrative Procedures

Q 15:12 What form does this authorization take?

Most state power of attorney, representation, and authorization forms are similar to federal Form 2848. Generally, the forms detail the powers granted to the representative with respect to specific time periods and taxes and allow for amendment and modification by the taxpayer. The states and their respective power of attorney or authorization forms are listed in the following table.

States Power of Attorney or Authorization Forms

State	*Required Form*
Alabama	Form 2848A
Alaska	Form 04-775
Arizona	Form 286
Arkansas	Power of Attorney
California	BOE-392
Colorado	Form 0145
Connecticut	Form LGL-001
District of Columbia	Accepts a copy of the federal Form 2848
Florida	Form DR-835
Georgia	Form RD-1061
Hawaii	Form N-848
Idaho	TC-00111
Illinois	Form IL-2848
Indiana	Form POA1
Kentucky	Federal Form 2848, or a written authorization to represent the corporation
Louisiana	Power of Attorney
Maine	Form 2848-ME
Massachusetts	Form M-2848
Michigan	Form 151
Minnesota	Rev 184
Mississippi	Accepts a copy of the federal Form 2848
Missouri	Accepts a copy of the federal Form 2848
Nebraska	Form 33
New Jersey	M-5008
New Mexico	Letter or DI-6
New York	POA-1
North Carolina	Accepts a copy of the federal Form 2848
North Dakota	Form 500
Ohio	Form TBOR-1
State	Required Form
Oklahoma	Accepts a copy of the federal Form 2848
Pennsylvania	Accepts a federal power of attorney form, Form 2848, or a written authorization to represent the corporation
Rhode Island	Form RI-2848
South Carolina	Form SC2848
Tennessee	Power of Attorney

State	*Required Form*
Texas	Form 00-750
Utah	Accepts a copy of the federal Form 2848
Virginia	PAR 101
West Virginia	WV-2848 and WV ARI-001
Wisconsin	Form A-222
Wyoming	Accepts a copy of the federal Form 2848

Chapter 16

Assessment and Appeals Process

Most sales and use tax audits end in assessment. It is important, therefore, for tax practitioners and taxpayers to understand the mechanics of how assessments are issued, the procedures for appealing assessments, and the administrative steps and alternatives with which the taxpayer is faced. Naturally, the procedures vary from state to state, and it is to these issues we turn in this chapter.

Assessment

Q 16:3 How long does the taxpayer have to respond to a sales and use tax assessment?

If a taxpayer wishes to appeal an assessment, she usually has only 10 to 90 days from the date of the notice to request a hearing. If the 10- to 90-day period has lapsed, the right to appeal is lost and the taxpayer must pay the assessment. To protest the assessment, the taxpayer must make the protest and request for hearing in writing.

Response Period

Time Period	*State*
10 days	Mississippi
15 days	Louisiana
20 days	Texas
30 days	Alabama, Arkansas, California, Colorado, District of Columbia, Georgia, Hawaii, Maine, Maryland, Massachusetts, Michigan, Nebraska, New Mexico, New York, North Carolina, North Dakota, Ohio, Oklahoma, Pennsylvania, Rhode Island, South Carolina, South Dakota, Tennessee, Utah, Virginia (for payment and 90 days for formal appeal), Washington, Wyoming
45 days	Arizona, Kentucky, Nevada
60 days	Connecticut, Florida, Illinois, Indiana, Iowa, Kansas, Minnesota, Missouri, Ohio, Vermont, West Virginia, Wisconsin
63 days	Idaho
90 days	New Jersey

Planning Point 16-2. In most states, once the appeal deadline has expired, the taxpayer forfeits its right to appeal. For taxpayers with several audits, it may be prudent to maintain a calendar of appeal deadlines for each audit to avoid missing one unnecessarily.

Statute of Limitations

Q 16:9 What is the statute of limitations period for sales and use taxes?

A state's sales and use tax statute of limitations establishes the length of time for which a taxpayer may file a refund claim or the state impose an assessment of tax.

Although the statute of limitations is frequently identical to the three-year federal statute of limitations for income tax assessments, a number of states provide for a longer period. These states are listed in the following table.

States with a Statute of Limitations Greater than Three Years

State	*Statute of Limitations*
Arizona	4 years
California	8-year statute of limitations if no return is filed
Idaho	7 years if no return is filed, and no time limit if the taxpayer has committed fraud
Illinois	3.5 years, with the period extended to 6.5 years for nonfilers, and no limit for those filing a fraudulent return
Kentucky	4 years
Maine	6-year limit applies if the tax liability was understated by 50 percent or more, and no time limit exists if there is fraud or a failure to file a return
Maryland	4 years
Michigan	4 years, and no limit for nonfilers
Minnesota	3.5 years, and 6.5 years if understated liability by 25 percent or more, and no limit for nonfilers
Missouri	5 years for nonfilers
Nebraska	5 years for nonfilers
Nevada	8-year statute of limitations if no return is filed
New Jersey	4 years
New Mexico	7 years for nonfilers
New York	indefinitely for nonfilers
North Dakota	6 years
Ohio	4 years
Rhode Island	6 years for nonfilers
South Carolina	6 years if the tax liability is understated by more than 25 percent; indefinitely for nonfilers
Tennessee	6 years for nonfilers
Texas	4 years
Vermont	6 years if the tax liability is understated by more than 20 percent; indefinitely for nonfilers or a fraudulent return
Virginia	6 years for nonfilers or a fraudulent return
Washington	5 years
West Virginia	indefinitely for nonfilers
Wisconsin	4 years

Chapter 17

Collection of Tax by Seller

Vendors doing business in a state are responsible for collecting and remitting sales tax upon their taxable sales of tangible personal property and select services. Although the tax is due from the purchaser, the state may assess the seller for any tax the seller should have collected but did not collect. If companies selling by mail order or through the Internet have physical presence in the state, they must also collect a state's sales and use tax. This chapter discusses the issues related to the collection of sales and use tax by a seller. Chapter 18 discusses collection of sales and use taxes by the state.

Passing On or Absorbing the Tax

Q 17:2 Must a seller pass the sales tax on to the buyer?

In 36 states, the sales tax must be passed on to the seller. The states include Alabama, Arkansas, Colorado, Connecticut, Florida, Georgia, Idaho, Indiana, Iowa, Kansas, Kentucky, Louisiana, Maine, Maryland, Massachusetts, Minnesota, Mississippi, Missouri, Nebraska, Nevada, New Jersey, New York, North Carolina, North Dakota, Ohio, Oklahoma, Pennsylvania, Rhode Island, Tennessee, Texas, Utah, Vermont, Virginia, West Virginia, Wisconsin, and Wyoming.

Sellers may absorb the sales tax in nine states: Arizona, California, Hawaii, Illinois, Michigan, New Mexico, South Carolina, South Dakota, and Washington.

Many states prohibit a vendor from absorbing the tax, that is, from adjusting the price to the consumer either through refund or credit memo. Absorption is illegal because most statutes require that the buyer *pay* and the seller *collect* the tax. Thus, issuing a refund or credit memo back to the buyer in the amount of sales tax collected may run afoul of anti-absorption laws. [Rudnick Bros. v. Johnson & Sons, 186 N.Y.S.2d 169 (1959)] However, a vendor is allowed to adjust his sales price. Unlike the general principle in income tax of "substance over form," in sales tax form generally takes precedence over substance.

Example 17-2. Jones Motor Co., a used-car dealership, runs a two-week advertising campaign saying that "if you buy the car, we pay the tax." Susan purchases a car for $10,000 plus 5 percent sales tax. Jones charges her the $10,000 and absorbs the $500 tax. This is illegal in states prohibiting absorption, and Susan can still be assessed the $500 tax by the state.

Example 17-3. Jones Motor Co., a used-car dealership, runs a two-week advertising campaign saying, "We will reduce the marked sales price of any car by the sales tax due." Susan picks out a car marked for sale at $10,000. Because 5 percent sales tax on $10,000 is $500, Jones Motor reduces the selling price by that amount and charges Susan $9,500 plus sales tax of $475. By reducing the selling price and still charging the tax, Jones Motor has not violated the state's anti-absorption statute.

Planning Point 17-3. To avoid potential problems with the absorption of tax, sellers should generally quote all prices as "not including applicable sales and use tax." Purchasers would then be put on notice that tax will be added to the selling price of the goods and services purchased. In addition, quoting prices without tax also avoids legal questions regarding the appropriate rate to charge when tax rates change.

Q 17:3 Must the sales tax be separately advertised or stated?

The sales tax must be separately stated in 29 states and the District of Columbia. There is no requirement for separate statement in

17 states. In 10 states, the sales tax need not be separately stated, although the seller is still required to pass the sales tax on to the consumer. There are 2 states that, while not requiring the pass-through of the sales tax to the consumer, do mandate a separate listing or advertising of the tax.

Sales Tax Pass-Through and Separately Stated Requirement

State	*Must Be Passed Through*	*Must Be Separately Stated*
Alabama	Yes	No
Arizona	No	Yes
Arkansas	Yes	No
California	No	No
Colorado	Yes	Yes
Connecticut	Yes	No
District of Columbia	Yes	Yes
Florida	Yes	Yes
Georgia	Yes	No
Hawaii	No	No
Idaho	Yes	Yes
Illinois	No	No
Indiana	Yes	Yes
Iowa	Yes	Yes
Kansas	Yes	Yes
Kentucky	Yes	Yes
Louisiana	Yes	Yes
Maine	Yes	No
Maryland	Yes	Yes
Massachusetts	Yes	Yes
Michigan	No	No
Minnesota	Yes	Yes
Mississippi	Yes	No
Missouri	Yes	Yes
Nebraska	Yes	Yes
Nevada	Yes	Yes
New Jersey	Yes	Yes
New Mexico	No	No
New York	Yes	Yes
North Carolina	Yes	Yes

State	*Must Be Passed Through*	*Must Be Separately Stated*
North Dakota	Yes	Yes
Ohio	Yes	No
Oklahoma	Yes	Yes
Pennsylvania	Yes	Yes
Rhode Island	Yes	No
South Carolina	No	Yes
South Dakota	No	No
Tennessee	Yes	Yes
Texas	Yes	Yes
Utah	Yes	Yes
Vermont	Yes	Yes
Virginia	Yes	Yes
Washington	No	No
West Virginia	Yes	No
Wisconsin	Yes	Yes
Wyoming	Yes	No

Planning Point 17-4. Vendors should quote the sales price as "plus tax" whenever possible. In states that hold that a quoted price includes the tax, such wording will protect the seller against assessments of amounts not recoverable from the buyer. In other states, this wording will avoid the expense and bother of a suit to recover the tax from the buyer. If competitive pressures make "lump-sum" quotes essential, separate billing of the tax may protect the seller in some states.

Collection by Out-of-State Sellers

Q 17:7 What activities of an out-of-state vendor would create a duty to collect state taxes?

According to the U.S. Supreme Court, a state can require use tax collection of any out-of-state vendor whose physical presence in the state is more than *de minimis*. [Quill v. North Dakota, 504 U.S. 298 (1992)] Many states, following the *Quill* decision, have broadly defined their "doing business" standards to include any activity beyond minimal physical presence. *Quill,* however, does not force a state to take a broad reading of "doing business." A state's requirements for nexus can be more narrow, but not broader, than *Quill*'s minimal physical presence rule. As a consequence, it is still important to look specifically at each state's interpretation of "doing business" to determine just what activities the state defines as creating nexus for sales and use tax.

In many states sales activities do or do not create nexus for sales and use tax. The activities include canvassing, hawking, peddling, having a sales or sample room, making mail-order sales, and distributing catalogs.

Thirty-three states and the District of Columbia hold that canvassing creates a collection responsibility for out-of-state vendors. Those states include Alabama, Arizona, Arkansas, California, Colorado, Connecticut, Idaho, Indiana, Iowa, Kansas, Kentucky, Maryland, Massachusetts, Michigan, Mississippi, Missouri, Nebraska, Nevada, New Jersey, New Mexico, New York, North Carolina, North Dakota, Ohio, Oklahoma, Rhode Island, South Dakota, Tennessee, Texas, Utah, West Virginia, Wisconsin, and Wyoming.

In Arkansas, Indiana, and Missouri, hawking will create a filing obligation for out-of-state vendors. (*Hawking* is a somewhat archaic word meaning to offer to sell by calling out in the street.)

Peddling is deemed to create sales and use tax nexus for out-of-state vendors in Arizona, Arkansas, Connecticut, Idaho, Iowa, Kansas, Kentucky, Maryland, Massachusetts, Michigan, Mississippi, Missouri, Nebraska, Nevada, New Jersey, New York, North Carolina, North Dakota, Ohio, Oklahoma, Rhode Island, South Dakota, Utah, West Virginia, and Wisconsin. Given the *Quill* decision (*see* Q. 17:6), it should be presumed that the states' use of the terms "canvassing," "hawking," and "peddling" all require physical presence. If not, it is doubtful that claiming nexus based on these activities would withstand constitutional scrutiny.

Setting up a sales or sample room will create sales and use tax nexus in 26 states and the District of Columbia (Alabama, California, Colorado, Connecticut, Idaho, Illinois, Indiana, Iowa, Kansas, Maine, Maryland, Michigan, Minnesota, Mississippi, Nebraska, Nevada, New Jersey, New York, North Carolina, Ohio, Rhode Island, South Dakota, Utah, Vermont, West Virginia, and Wyoming).

And despite the Supreme Court's rulings in *National Bellas Hess* and *Quill* (*see* Q 17:6), in Alabama, an out-of-state vendor mailing catalogs into their state has created an obligation to collect the state's use tax. Alabama also claims that telemarketing calls into the state create nexus. In this belief, it is not alone. Other states holding the same position include Arizona, Nebraska, Tennessee, and Wisconsin.

Nine states hold that distribution of mail-order catalogs via drop shipment from within the state is sufficient to create nexus. They include Alabama, Colorado, Massachusetts, Michigan, Mississippi, Nebraska, Oklahoma, Pennsylvania, and Tennessee.

Inventories have been particularly troublesome for tax administrators and preparers alike. Specifically there are at least four activities unique to inventory ownership that raise questions of nexus. The activities are consignment, delivery, distribution, and storage.

Six states (Arkansas, Indiana, Maine, Missouri, New Jersey, and North Carolina) report that consignment of inventories into the state creates a use-tax-filing obligation.

The U.S. Supreme Court ruled in *Miller Bros.* that delivery of goods purchased in Delaware and delivered in company trucks to customers in Maryland did not create a use-tax-filing obligation in Maryland. [Miller Bros. v. Maryland, 347 U.S. 340 (1954)] Many state tax administrators believe that the Court's application of due process in *Quill* has superseded the holding in *Miller Bros.* Their belief has been supported by recent state court cases. [*See, e.g.*, Good's Furniture House v. Iowa, 382 N.W.2d 145 (Iowa 1986), *cert. denied,* 479 U.S. 817 (1986); John Swenson Granite v. State, No. CV-93-214 (Me. Jan. 10, 1996); Brown's Furniture v. Wagner, 171 Ill. 2d 410 (1996), *cert. denied,* 519 U.S. 866 (1996).] As a consequence, 41 states and the District of Columbia now hold that delivery of goods into their state by any means other than mail or common carrier creates nexus for sales and use tax. The states include Arizona, Arkansas, California, Colorado, Connecticut, Georgia, Idaho, Illinois, Indiana, Iowa, Kansas, Kentucky, Louisiana, Maine, Maryland, Massachusetts, Michigan, Minnesota, Mississippi, Missouri, Nebraska, Nevada, New Jersey, New Mexico, New York, North Carolina, North Dakota, Ohio, Oklahoma, Pennsylvania, Rhode Island, South Carolina, South Dakota, Tennessee, Texas, Utah, Vermont, Virginia, West Virginia, Wisconsin, and Wyoming.

Forty-one states and the District of Columbia hold that maintaining a distribution house or distributing inventories within the state generates a use tax liability for out-of-state vendors. Those states include Alabama, Arkansas, California, Colorado, Connecticut, Florida, Georgia, Idaho, Illinois, Indiana, Iowa, Kansas, Kentucky, Louisiana, Maine, Maryland, Michigan, Minnesota, Mississippi, Missouri, Nebraska, Nevada, New Jersey, New Mexico, New York, North Carolina, North Dakota, Ohio, Oklahoma, Pennsylvania, Rhode Island, South Carolina, South Dakota, Tennessee, Texas, Utah, Vermont, Virginia, West Virginia, Wisconsin, and Wyoming.

Some states have gone so far as to claim that advertising on local and national media or by satellite television creates nexus. Most commentators find it preposterous that advertising, absent any other activity or physical presence, can create nexus. Nevertheless, Alabama, Arizona, Nebraska, New Mexico, Pennsylvania, South Carolina, Utah, Virginia, and West Virginia all report that advertising in local media or on satellite television creates nexus.

For the majority of states and the District of Columbia, advertising alone is simply not sufficient to create nexus. These states include Arkansas, California [*see* JS&A Group, Inc. v. California Bd. of Equalization, No. 969816 (Cal. Ct. App. Feb. 10, 1997)], Colorado, Connecticut, Florida, Georgia, Hawaii, Idaho, Illinois, Indiana, Iowa, Kansas, Kentucky, Louisiana, Maine, Maryland, Massachusetts, Michigan [*see* Scholastic Book Clubs v. Department of Revenue, 223 Mich. App. 576 (1997)], Minnesota, Mississippi, Missouri, Nevada, New Jersey, New York, North Carolina, North Dakota, Ohio, Oklahoma, Rhode Island, South Dakota, Tennessee, Texas, Vermont, Washington, Wisconsin, and Wyoming. Claims that advertising, without any other activity, will create nexus are simply not sustained by any reading of *Quill.* Nexus has been found where there is physical presence coupled with advertising. [Good's Furniture House v. Iowa, 382 N.W.2d 145 (Iowa 1986), *cert. denied,* 479 U.S. 817 (1987)] In *Good's Furniture,* the Iowa Supreme Court held that intensive television advertising coupled with significant Iowa sales and the delivery of merchandise in Good's own trucks was "substantial presence" sufficient to justify nexus. The Vermont Supreme Court took a similar position in *Rowe-Genereux, Inc. v. Vermont Department of Taxes,* 138 Vt. 130 (1980).

Most states hold that installation and maintenance work on tangible personal property performed by third parties will create nexus for the out-of-state vendor that contracted with the parties. The states taking this position include Alabama, Arizona, Arkansas, California (installation but not necessarily maintenance), Colorado, Connecticut, Georgia, Hawaii, Idaho, Illinois (if the third party is an agent for the out-of-state vendor), Iowa, Kansas, Kentucky, Louisiana, Maine, Maryland, Massachusetts (depending on the facts), Michigan, Minnesota, Mississippi, Nebraska, New Jersey (depending on the facts), New Mexico, New York (possibly, as it is currently under review), North Carolina, North Dakota, Ohio, Oklahoma (depending on the facts), Pennsylvania, Rhode Island, South Carolina, South Dakota, Texas, Utah, Vermont, Washington, and Wyoming. The only states that find third-party installation and maintenance work insufficient to create nexus are Florida, Indiana, Missouri, Nevada, Virginia, West Virginia, and Wisconsin.

Contracting with an in-state printing company may create nexus if the printer stores the printed material for the out-of-state vendor or the vendor makes occasional visits to the printer. No state claims that mere contracting alone with no other activity in the state will create nexus for the out-of-state vendor. When the printer stores the printed materials for the out-of-state vendor, 27 states and the District of Columbia consider this physical presence sufficient to create nexus (Alabama, Arizona, California, Colorado, Georgia, Hawaii, Idaho, Maine, Maryland, Michigan, Mississippi, Nebraska, Nevada, New Jersey, New Mexico, North Carolina, North Dakota, Oklahoma, Rhode Island, South Dakota, Texas, Utah, Vermont, Virginia (if stored for use in Virginia), Washington, West Virginia, and Wyoming). Connecticut and Massachusetts report that occasional visits by the vendor's personnel might trigger nexus. Sixteen states do not consider contracting with an in-state printer or occasional visits sufficient activity to trigger nexus. They include Arkansas, Florida, Georgia, Indiana, Iowa, Kansas, Kentucky, Louisiana, Minnesota, Missouri, New York (currently under review), Ohio, Pennsylvania, South Carolina, Tennessee, and Wisconsin.

Planning Point 17-6. The diversity among the states makes the management of nexus extremely complex for state tax managers. In order to monitor the situation, the state tax manager needs to be in regular communications with areas, such as sales, marketing, service, and manufacturing, that are likely to have activities that could affect a company's nexus in a particular state. Periodically re-evaluating the taxpayer's nexus position in each jurisdiction can reduce exposure to unpaid taxes and avoid unnecessary overpayment of taxes that may be difficult to recover at a later date.

Chapter 19

Penalties

States impose penalties to encourage compliance, to discourage delinquent filing, and to raise revenue. As a consequence, there exists a wide range of possible penalties, including penalties for late filing, late payment, negligence, willful negligence, fraud, etc. Every state with a sales and use tax levies penalties for delinquent filing or nonfiling. The severity of the penalty assessed varies widely from state to state. This chapter discusses the penalties and interest applicable to late sales and use tax filings.

Penalties

Q 19:7 Which states allow a prompt-payment discount?

Many states offer vendor discounts, often called prompt-payment discounts, to encourage compliance. The discounts help compensate the seller for the inconvenience of serving as the state's collection agent and act as an incentive to timely filing. The discounts range in amount from one-half of 1 percent to $3\frac{1}{3}$ percent of the tax due. Most states either cap the vendor's fee or reduce the percentage refunded above a certain amount. The discount is not available on late returns. States offering a vendor discount are Alabama, Arkansas, Colorado, Florida, Georgia, Illinois, Indiana, Kansas, Kentucky, Louisiana, Maryland, Michigan, Mississippi, Missouri, Nevada, New York, North Dakota, Ohio, Oklahoma, Pennsylvania, Rhode Island, South Carolina, Texas, Utah, Virginia, Wisconsin, and Wyoming.

Interest

Q 19:11 What rate of interest is used by the states?

The interest rates applicable to state taxes vary not only from state to state but also within a single state between refunds (overpayments) and amounts due (underpayments). The annual rates range from a low of 2 percent in California on overpayments to a high of 15 percent in Louisiana on amounts due. The manner in which and frequency with which states set their interest rates also varies. While many states have set rates determined by statute, other states provide for floating rates tied to the prime interest rate or the federal short-term rates plus a certain percentage. The following states report using a single rate for both overpayments and underpayments: Arizona, Arkansas, Colorado, Florida, Georgia, Hawaii, Idaho, Iowa, Kansas, Kentucky, Maine, Massachusetts, Michigan, Minnesota, Mississippi, Missouri, Nebraska, New Mexico, North Carolina, Ohio, Oklahoma, Pennsylvania, Rhode Island, South Carolina, South Dakota, Tennessee, Texas, Utah, Vermont, and West Virginia.

Sixteen states and the District of Columbia use different rates for overpayments and underpayments, with higher rates applied to under- than to overpayments: Alabama, California, Connecticut, Illinois, Indiana, Louisiana, Maryland, Nevada, New Jersey, New York, North Dakota, Virginia, Washington, Wisconsin, and Wyoming.

The following chart lists the rates (effective January 1, 2003), how frequently they are adjusted, and the method by which they are determined:

State Interest Rates

State	*Rate (Overpayments/ Underpayments)*	*Frequency of Adjustment*	*How Rates Are Determined*
Alabama	5%	Quarterly	Use federal rate
Arizona	5%	Quarterly	Use federal rates
Arkansas	10%	No set interval	Set by statute

State	*Rate (Overpayments/ Underpayments)*	*Frequency of Adjustment*	*How Rates Are Determined*
California	2%/9%	Semiannually	Overpayments: use 13-week Treasury bill rate Underpayments: use federal underpayment rate + 3%
Colorado	8%	Annually	Use prime rate + 3%
Connecticut	NR/1% per month	No set interval	Use fixed rate
District of Columbia	6%/10%	No set interval	Use fixed rate
Florida	5%	Semiannually	Set by statute
Georgia	12%	No set interval	Set by statute
Hawaii	8%	No set interval	Set by statute
Idaho	5%	Annually	Use federal mid-term rate as of October 15 of prior year + 2%
Illinois	Varies	Semiannually	Underpayments: use federal rate
Indiana	4%/6%	Annually	Overpayments: use average yield by state + 2%Underpayments: use average yield by state
Iowa	7%	Annually	Use 12-month average of prime rate + 2%
Kansas	7%	Annually	Federal rate on July 1 of prior year + 1%
Kentucky	5%	Annually	Use prime rate in October
Louisiana	4.5%/15%	No set interval Annually	Overpayments: use fixed rate Underpayments: use average 52-week Treasury bill rate as of September 30 of prior year + 2%, minimum 7%, maximum 14%
Maine	7%	Annually	Use conventional rate for unsecured commercial loans on first day of business preceding October
Maryland	13%	Annually	Overpayments: use average investment yield on state funds for prior fiscal year + 2% Underpayments: use greater of 13% or prime + 3%
Massachusetts	6%	Quarterly	Use federal short-term rate + 4%
Michigan	5.8%	Semiannually	Use adjusted prime rate + 1%
Minnesota	5%	Annually	Use prime rate rounded to nearest full percentage point
Mississippi	1% per month	No set interval	Use fixed rate

State	*Rate (Overpayments/ Underpayments)*	*Frequency of Adjustment*	*How Rates Are Determined*
Missouri	5%	Annually	Use September's prime rate
Nebraska	6%	Biannually	Use fixed rate
Nevada	6%/12%	No set interval	Use fixed rate
New Jersey	4.25%/7.25%	Quarterly	Overpayments: use prime rate Underpayments: use prime rate + 3%
New Mexico	15%	No set interval	Use fixed rate
New York	6%/14%	Quarterly	Overpayments: use federal short-term rate + 2% Underpayments: use 12% or rate set by Commissioner
North Carolina	6%	Semiannually	Use fixed rate
North Dakota	10%/12%	No set interval	Use fixed rate
Ohio	6%	Annually	Use federal short-term rate + 3%
Oklahoma	15%	No set interval	Use fixed rate
Pennsylvania	5%	Annually	Use federal rate on January 1
Rhode Island	12%	Annually	Use October prime rate + 2%, minimum 12%
South Carolina	5%	Quarterly	Use fixed rate
South Dakota	15%	No set interval	Use fixed rate
Tennessee	8.75%	Annually	Use fixed rate
Texas	5.25%	Annually	Use prime rate + 1%
Utah	5%	Annually	Use fixed rate
Vermont	6%	Annually	Use average prime rate during prior 12 months
Virginia	7%	Quarterly	Overpayments: use federal overpayment rate Underpayments: use federal underpayment rate + 2%
Washington	5%	Annually	Overpayments: use average federal short-term rate for preceding calendar year + 1% Underpayments: use average federal short-term rate for preceding calendar year + 2%
West Virginia	8%/9.5%	Semiannually	Use prime rate, but not less than 8%
Wisconsin	9%/12%	No set interval	Use fixed rate
Wyoming	9.32%	Annually	Use average prime rate during the preceding fiscal year + 4%

Q 19:12 Is interest compounded?

Most states use simple interest. Specifically, 33 states use simple interest. The states include California, Colorado, Connecticut, Georgia, Hawaii, Idaho, Illinois, Indiana, Iowa, Kansas, Kentucky, Louisiana, Maryland, Michigan, Minnesota, Mississippi, Missouri, Nebraska, Nevada, New Mexico, North Dakota, Ohio, Oklahoma, Pennsylvania, Rhode Island, South Dakota, Tennessee, Texas, Utah, Vermont, Virginia, Wisconsin, and Wyoming. The rest of the states and the District of Columbia (daily) use compound interest. They are Alabama (daily), Arizona (annually), Arkansas (daily), Florida (daily), Maine (monthly), Massachusetts (daily), New Jersey (not reported), New York (daily), North Carolina (daily), South Carolina (daily), Washington (daily), and West Virginia (daily).

Chapter 21

Sales Tax Reform and the Streamlined Sales Tax Project

From the moment any tax is introduced there begin cries to reform it, to make it simpler, fairer, and more efficient. Sales tax, like income tax, is always in want of reform. Since the introduction of sales taxes in the 1930s there have been vast changes in technology, communication, transportation, and manufacturing, which directly impact transaction taxes in ways unfelt by taxes on income. Changes in technology and communication, for example, raise fundamental questions about the definition of concepts central to sales and use tax such as *tangible personal property* and *sale*. In this chapter we address the most recent of these reform attempts, the Streamlined Sales Tax Project (SSTP). (Given the ongoing nature of the SSTP, its current status can be tracked at its web site at: http://www.geocities.com/streamlined2000/.)

The Streamlined Sales Tax Project

Q 21:16 What is the Streamlined Sales Tax Project's timeline?

On November 12, 2002, the 35 Streamlined Sales Tax Implementing States ratified the final version of the Streamlined Sales and Use Tax Agreement. Thirty of the 35 states voted for the agreement. Four member states were absent and Maryland abstained due to its concerns regarding rounding. (One Maryland official said that the rounding provision would cost the state $20 million in tax revenue.) The November 12 vote ended the first phase of the SSTP process.

The second phase of the SSTP began in January with attempts by the 35 implementing states to introduce model SSTP legislation in their respective state legislatures. Ten states representing at least 20 percent of the population of states that impose a sales tax must adopt the Streamlined Sales and Use Tax Agreement before it can become effective. As of July 31, 2003, 19 states had enacted conforming legislation adopting the Agreement. The 19 states include Arkansas, Indiana, Iowa, Kansas, Kentucky, Minnesota, Nebraska, Nevada, North Carolina, North Dakota, Ohio, Oklahoma, South Dakota, Tennessee, Texas, Utah, Vermont, West Virginia, and Wyoming. These states represent more than the 20 percent of the population needed to make the Agreement effective.

While the SSTP victory is close, it is not certain. The Agreement requires that for a state to count as one of the 10 conforming states, its legislation must be substantially compliant with the various provisions of the Agreement. Since even among the 19 states that have currently enacted conforming legislation, there remain some differences in both substance and procedure, it is certain that there will be debate over what constitutes "substantial compliance."

Supporters of the SSTP hope to reach the 20 percent threshold before the expiration of the Internet Tax Freedom Act (ITFA) on November 1, 2003. ITFA prohibited state and local jurisdictions from (1) passing discriminatory taxes with respect to sales over the Internet and (2) charging sales tax on Internet access fees. Jurisdictions that had been taxing Internet access fees prior to October 1, 1998, were exempted from the Act. Legislation has already been introduced in Congress to extend ITFA. The Internet Tax Nondiscrimination Act (H.R. 49) would make the prohibitions of ITFA against taxing Internet access permanent as well as eliminate the "grandfather" clause allowing states and cities taxing Internet access prior to October 1, 1998, to continue to do so.

SSTP participants hope that by simplifying sales tax compliance they can persuade Congress to pass legislation in the fall of 2003 requiring the collection of sales tax by remote sellers, whether they sell over the Internet or by catalog through the mail. Thus, the political battle in the fall of 2003 over the renewal of ITFA and the supporters of the SSTP will be the most significant issue in state and local taxation in several years. Details of the SSTP and its progress can be tracked at their website: www.streamlinedsalestax.org.

Internal Revenue Code

[References are to supplement question numbers.]

IRC §

Internal Revenue Service Releases

[References are to supplement question numbers.]

Revenue Procedures

Revenue Rulings

Cases

[References are to supplement question numbers.]

C

D

E

Y

Index

[References are to supplement question numbers.]

L

M

N

O

P

R

S

T

U

V

W